Women Activists in the Fight for
Georgia School Desegregation, 1958–1961

Women Activists in the Fight for Georgia School Desegregation, 1958–1961

REBECCA H. DARTT

McFarland & Company, Inc., Publishers
Jefferson, North Carolina, and London

LIBRARY OF CONGRESS CATALOGUING-IN-PUBLICATION DATA

Dartt, Rebecca H.
    Women activists in the fight for Georgia school desegregation,
1958–1961 / Rebecca H. Dartt.
        p.   cm.
    Includes bibliographical references and index.

    ISBN 978-0-7864-3843-3
    softcover : 50# alkaline paper

    1. School integration — Georgia — History — 20th century.
2. Public schools — Georgia — History — 20th century.
3. African Americans — Education — Georgia — History — 20th
century.   4. Women — Georgia — Political activity — History —
20th century.   I. Title.
LC214.22.G46D37   2008
379.2'63 — dc22   2008022974

British Library cataloguing data are available

Cover photograph © 2007 Shutterstock

Manufactured in the United States of America

*McFarland & Company, Inc., Publishers
  Box 611, Jefferson, North Carolina 28640
  www.mcfarlandpub.com*

To all the women in Georgia
who knew the value of public education
and worked to preserve it
1958–1961

Acknowledgments

I am indebted to the many women of HOPE who shared their memories with me. It was my great pleasure to listen and marvel at their stories. I want to thank Muriel Lokey for being a faithful correspondent during the years of writing this book and for her wise comments; Fran Breeden gave me a vivid picture of what it was like starting the HOPE journey; I found myself mesmerized by Maxine Friedman's spicy, "Tell it like it is" rendition of those times; Janet Ferguson provided insight into the role her husband, Harry Boyte, played in the early days of HOPE; Beverly Long and Frances Pauley spoke of scary and funny times as they traveled around the state; Nan Pendergrast's unique contributions to HOPE lent an authentic dimension; and I was amazed at the courage of Phyllis and Judge James Barrow in taking a controversial stand for open schools in the explosive aftermath of riots at the University of Georgia. Professor Paul T. Mertz's interview with Betty Harris provided many interesting and important details in the HOPE story.

I am grateful to Madelyn Nix-Beamen and Thomas Welch, for sharing their experiences as transfer students with me.

Although this story centers on women and their role in HOPE, for they were the heavy lifters, there were many men who contributed their special skills and knowledge to the effort. Harry Boyte made a significant contribution to HOPE's beginning; James Dorsey offered legal advice to HOPE; Muggsy Smith, James Mackay, and Hamilton Lokey represented open schools in and outside the General Assembly. Many other men served on advisory boards.

I am indebted to Jeff Roche for his comprehensive book, *Restructured Resistance: The Sibley Commission and the Politics of Desegregation in Georgia,* which became my source for this historic committee, and its effects on Georgia politics and the public school crisis.

The Atlanta History Center, with its vast reservoir of information, was used extensively. The Auburn Avenue Research Library on African-American Culture and History under the able guidance of Carolyn Clark rendered an invaluable service for this project as well. My appreciation is extended to Jill Severn and Sheryl Vogt from the Richard Russell Library for Political Research and Studies, The University of Georgia Libraries.

I would like to thank Emory University for sponsoring a HOPE symposium in March 2000, an occasion to revisit the important events during Georgia's public school desegregation era and to honor the men and women whose contributions made the difference in the historic struggle.

I offer my sincere appreciation to Michael McErvin, whose editing skills enhanced the telling of this story.

I am deeply grateful to my husband, George Dartt, who saved me hours of frustration by solving computer problems and for believing in me and the project.

Table of Contents

Table of Contents

Preface

One morning in the fall of 1958, a group of Atlanta mothers came together for coffee with one topic in mind: the reality that Georgia schools might shut down. The United States Supreme Court decision of 1954, *Brown v. Board of Education,* had outlawed the separate-but-equal formula of public education practiced in the South for decades. On the heels of that historic change in national policy, the Georgia General Assembly enacted a series of massive resistance laws to oppose the federal mandate, and in his 1958 campaign for governor, Ernest Vandiver promised voters that no black child would enter a white school under his administration. The Atlanta women feared children across the state, including their own, would be the real losers in the battle. That first neighborhood meeting grew to be a movement, and chapters were organized in most of the 159 counties in the state. The Atlanta women named their group Help Our Public Education (HOPE, Inc.). They embarked on a monumental journey that none of them could have imagined from its modest beginnings over coffee. In fact, we have these women to thank for moving the school crisis from politics-as-usual to instigating a profound change in the way the public viewed the problem. Most of the women were not starry-eyed idealists, however. Their goal was two-fold: to comply with the court order to desegregate without violence and to keep public schools open.

Women Activists in the Fight for Georgia School Desegregation includes historical background to show how past policies and events in Georgia

1

evolved into the situation the state faced at the time that HOPE was organized. This portion of the book demonstrates how long it takes a society to move beyond traumatic upheavals. This was certainly true for Georgians after the devastation of the Civil War and the punitive aftermath of Reconstruction. Memories are long, and entrenched beliefs die hard. Old-time Georgia politics set the stage for this battle, but in the end, politicians playing off these old memories lost credibility. It would not be long before the Georgia power brokers shifted from rural enclaves to the more progressive urban centers.

A primary purpose in writing this book was to illustrate that ordinary citizens in a democracy can change the course of history without violence, and in spite of entrenched beliefs. To paraphrase Margaret Mead, it takes only a small number of people to make a profound difference to our social fabric. We all benefit from experiencing an uplifting story of Americans who, putting their faith in our best democratic values, changed the culture for the better. However, this book is not only an important telling of a portion of history that too often goes untold, but a virtual primer for any grassroots activist or student of oral history.

I grew up in Decatur, Georgia, when segregation of blacks and whites was taken for granted, but at home, my mother, Betty Harris, exposed us to a different point of view. She made it clear that prejudice against blacks was wrong. She was one of the first organizers of inter-racial Girl Scout camps in the Atlanta area; she spearheaded joint events between her Central Congregational Church and the Congregational Church in the black community; she joined the few other whites on Atlanta's Human Relations Council; and she worked for progressive political candidates. By the time she was involved in HOPE as its executive director, I had left the South for college and then a job. Her letters were filled with enthusiasm regarding her work with HOPE as she shared with me an inside view of this exciting and precarious time. When I came home for visits, I often accompanied her to committee meetings, to the capital, and on the day in 1961 when black students entered white high schools for the first time, I joined others in the home of a HOPE volunteer to watch Northside High integrate. I will always remember the jubilation of that historic day.

Based on factual material found in library special collections, books, newspapers, interview transcripts, symposiums and forum speeches, and upon my taped interviews with HOPE leaders, this book is intended to honor my mother and the other exceptional women who made HOPE a success.

Chapter 1

To Break the Silence

We must not let the destroyers of constitutional government, the Communists and other outside interests close our schools, harm our children and disrupt racial harmony.... Please dear Georgians do not work or support any group that is trying to integrate our public schools.[1]

— Lester Maddox

The white, upscale area in north Atlanta was a picture postcard of beautiful homes, surrounded by manicured lawns, towering magnolias, and azalea gardens. Among the lavish properties of the very wealthy and powerful, however, lived families of more modest means, who were, nevertheless, privileged by any standard. The peaceful setting did not reflect how Northside mothers were feeling in the fall of 1958. They were worried about their children's schools.

Families, friends, and neighbors avoided mentioning the school question because it involved the possibility of black children mixing with whites — a cultural taboo ingrained in the Southern mind. The question of race, let alone the intermixing thereof, was filled with much raw emotion and was not a safe topic in polite company. Segregationists drowned out more moderate voices in the public discourse, but too worried to remain silent, some Northside mothers talked quietly when they picked up their children from school or Scouts. "What's going to happen? Where will our kids go if the schools close?"

Atlanta papers had been awash with news of Ernest Vandiver's gubernatorial campaign against the current arch-segregationist governor, Marvin

Griffin. Vandiver had been considered a moderate on racial issues until Griffin spread the word that Vandiver's campaign had allowed whites and blacks to stand in the same line at a Valdosta barbecue. Thereafter, Vandiver based his stump speeches on the defense of segregation and the "Georgia way of life," by adopting the motto: "No, not one." He pledged no Negro child would enter a white school in Georgia while he was governor.[2] He warned his audiences that if the federal courts ordered desegregation in Georgia it would be the end of public education for all children.

Ernest Vandiver was elected on the segregation issue, solidifying the already defiant position taken by Georgia's political machine in reaction to the Supreme Court's 1954 *Brown v. Board of Education* decision. The historic move to end public school segregation came after years of court battles in the South over other issues of inequality.

This slow process of righting the wrongs of the past began with President Truman's 1948 Executive Order to end segregation in the military. The NAACP (National Association for the Advancement of Colored People) recognized that the order to desegregate the military signaled an emerging social change in the country. They seized the opportunity to attack other instances of racial injustice, especially in the deep South. NAACP lawyers adopted a pragmatic strategy in court challenges. Rather than attack the separate-but-equal doctrine, the legal team went to court in Jim Crow states to demand that public facilities for blacks be raised to the standards of those for whites. It was common knowledge that facilities for blacks were markedly inferior to those for whites (e.g., public restrooms). In the early 1950s, southern politicians began to feel the effects of court decisions in favor of the NAACP regarding the equality of public facilities, which also brought about some upgrading of public schools for blacks. It was during this process that the NAACP managed to force an important breakthrough at the higher end of the educational ladder.

The so-called border states (Maryland, Missouri, Delaware, Kentucky) had been paying tuition for blacks to attend out-of-state professional schools and universities. A state court in Maryland held that the Constitution's equality standard could not be met by using this strategy. The option of establishing a law school at Maryland's black state college would have been prohibitive in cost, so the remaining alternative was to lower the color bar. Court-ordered desegregation of graduate schools followed in other border states.[3]

Some of the best trained young black lawyers on the NAACP legal team had received their Ivy League education with tuition grants from border states. Ironically, Jim Crow laws had given young black students the means to challenge the long-standing principle of white supremacy.

Because of this landmark change in higher education policy regarding race in the late 1940s, Thurgood Marshall, the head of the NAACP Legal Defense and Education Fund, began in 1950 to advocate a new strategy in litigation — a head-on fight to end school segregation at the public school level. Marshall, an imposing figure who stood tall and erect, spoke with extraordinary confidence after the strategy session: "We are going to insist on nonsegregation in American education from top to bottom — from law school to kindergarten."[4] His colleagues, both white and black lawyers, were stunned at this radical plan. They admired Marshall's boldness for they knew that they did not have the courage to promote such a plan.

NAACP lawyers started with five public school cases involving the range of segregation laws in force: Delaware, *Belton v. Gebhart;* Kansas, *Brown v. Board of Education*; South Carolina, *Briggs v. Elliot;* Virginia, *Davis v. County School Board of Prince Edward County*; and Washington, D.C., *Bolling v. C. Melvin Sharpe.* When the cases finally reached the Supreme Court, they were combined and provided the rationale for the 1954 ruling whose title, *Brown v. Board of Education,* came from the Topeka, Kansas, case that was the first on the list to be filed on appeal. The *Brown* case stemmed from a third-grader, Linda Brown, being forced to take a long bus ride past a closer neighborhood school that had denied her enrollment because she was black. Her father filed a suit against the Topeka Board of Education claiming racial discrimination.

The Virginia case highlighted some of the more deplorable conditions of black schools in the rural South. *Davis v. County School Board of Prince Edward County* came about after a courageous 16-year-old student named Barbara Rose Johns organized a student strike at the R. R. Moton High School in Farmville, Virginia, in April of 1951. Johns forged notes to teachers telling them to bring their students to the auditorium for a special announcement. When the students assembled, she took the stage and persuaded them to strike as a protest against poor school conditions. Students did not have a gymnasium, cafeteria or teachers' restrooms, and there were no desks or blackboards. Due to overcrowding, some students took classes in a decrepit school bus. The school's requests for adequate facilities and supplies were always denied by an all-white school board.

Over 450 students walked out and marched to the homes of school board members, who refused to see them. Their two-week protest lifted students' morale but only briefly. Prince Edward County eventually closed all schools — white and black — rather than integrate them. The schools remained closed from 1959 to 1964.[5]

Thurgood Marshall and his NAACP legal team successfully attacked the "separate-but-equal" doctrine established in the *Plessy v. Ferguson* decision of 1896. The Supreme Court ruled in the previous century that Homer Plessy of New Orleans, who was one-eighth Negro, could be legally forced to ride in a segregated coach for Negroes. The opinion read: "If one race be inferior to the other socially, the Constitution of the United States cannot put them on the same plane."[6] Fifty-eight years later the social climate had changed sufficiently for the NAACP to argue before the Supreme Court that the discriminatory nature of racial segregation "violates the 14th amendment to the United States Constitution, which guarantees all citizens equal protection of the laws." The Warren Court agreed unanimously with the NAACP and the unity on the Court added weight to their position on equality. The *Brown v. Board of Education* landmark decision on May 17, 1954 was celebrated by black Americans as a huge victory for justice. White segregationists bitterly opposed the decision.

The Supreme Court issued *Brown II* in 1955, which constituted the implementation order that placed enforcement of school desegregation in the hands of federal judges in the South and included the vague directive "with all deliberate speed."[7]

Immediately after the May decision, Judge Elbert Tuttle of the Fifth Circuit declared: "They'll (southern states) fall in line."[8] He could not have been more wrong.

Georgia politicians would not fade quietly into the night as Tuttle had predicted. Their voices rang loud and clear from podiums across the state as they proclaimed their outrage at being told by the federal government how to run their state's affairs. They worked quickly to pass a state referendum to amend Article VIII of the state Constitution of 1945, which read: "The provision of an adequate education for the citizens shall be a primary obligation of the State of Georgia, the expense of which shall be provided for by taxation. Separate schools shall be provided for the white and colored races."[9]

The Georgia League of Women Voters ran a vigorous campaign against passage of this referendum, which would permit distribution of public funds to private citizens for educational purposes: "Notwithstanding any other provision of this Constitution, the General Assembly may by law provide for grants of state, county or municipal funds to citizens of the state for educational purposes, in discharge of all obligation of the state to provide adequate education for its citizens."[10] The 1954 amendment to Article VIII was narrowly ratified in November of 1954 (210,488 to 181,148), six months after the *Brown* decision. In other words, this amendment made it possible for the state to hand over monies to private citizens to run their own schools in the event of a court desegregation order, which negated the state's responsibility to provide education for all its citizens.

The Georgia General Assembly also passed resistance laws to further thwart the desegregation of public schools. These laws dictated that all public schools in the state would close if one white school admitted one black child, and "every school" included the state university system.

Some of the Northside mothers had moved to Atlanta from the Midwest and the Northeast and these women spoke of closing schools as preposterous: "Atlanta with no public schools? That's crazy. Somebody will make lawmakers come to their senses."

In the fall of 1958, as these women began to share information and their alarm with one another, they were aware that the battle over the desegregation of schools had hit home with a local lawsuit. The previous January, twenty-seven black parents, represented by the NAACP, sued the Atlanta Board of Education for discrimination in the city schools. The case was moving slowly through the court system. Federal District judges Frank

A. Hooper and Boyd Sloan were assigned the case. Most court observers realized that the state was on a collision course with federal law. It was a fight of historic proportions with Atlanta as the battleground.

Muriel Lokey was not so sure some outside party would make politicians come to their senses and save the schools. Muriel had grown up in Tacoma, Washington. She married Hamilton (Ham) Lokey, an Atlanta native, and moved to the city as a young bride after the Second World War. By the mid–1950s, she had adopted the city as her own.

Ham Lokey, a prominent Atlanta lawyer, had served in the legislature and cast the one vote against the massive resistance bill in 1956. He knew enough about Georgia politics to realize the state faced a monumental crisis. With the "good ole boys" from rural counties dictating policy in the statehouse and legislature, Lokey was not optimistic. The Lokeys were a popular couple — Ham the loquacious southerner, and Muriel attractively supportive of her husband with a strong and independent mind of her own. She tended to get things done without any fuss.

The Lokeys had five children, four of whom were in public school and the youngest was a four-month-old baby. Muriel could not imagine anything so dreadful as having the schools close. She had to do something. She called a friend, Maxine Friedman, who had moved with her husband and children to Atlanta from New York six years before. Maxine had worked in public relations in New York City.

The two women talked on the phone and held brief conversations before and after their children's school events. Maxine, new to Georgia politics, could not fathom how a growing city like Atlanta could close its schools. However, Muriel, whose husband knew state politics through and through, tried to open Maxine's eyes to the Georgia reality. She told Maxine that everything in the state was decided by "the country boys," but Maxine persisted in arguing that Atlanta was full of educated people, that the schools would close "over my dead body."

The two women each called two more friends and asked them to call two friends apiece, and not long after, a group of women gathered in Muriel's living room over morning coffee. Nan Pendergrast, a member of a prominent Atlanta family going back to the Civil War, attended this first meeting. She had seen the sign, WE WANT PUBLIC SCHOOLS, on the fender of Maxine Friedman's car when picking up her children at Margaret Mitchell grammar school and immediately became involved. One woman interrupted the discussion as she clicked her cup onto the saucer. "You mean," she said, raising her voice, "Y'all are in favor of keeping the schools open and mixed!"[11] The disgruntled woman stalked out. The rest of the women stayed, vowing to spread the word and to bring more people together in the service of keeping Georgia's schools open.

They met again over coffee in Muriel's living room several days later and this time more women joined them. The group decided each person would again call two more friends.

The third gathering was an evening affair and more women came, with some bringing their husbands. Now it was time to ask the big question: What could they do to keep the schools open?

The manner in which other southern states had handled the school desegregation crisis was an alarming backdrop to those gathered in the Lokey's living room in October 1958. The fight in Little Rock, Arkansas, had rocked the nation the previous year. An angry mob of whites, protesting the entry of black students to Central High School in Little Rock, was caught on television screaming, "We don't want no niggers in our schools" and other inflammatory statements. The scene had erupted out of hardball politics from a political battle in which Arkansas Governor Orval Faubus had first floundered in the face of lingering racism and ultimately surrendered to it.

When the *Brown* decision came down, Faubus stated his belief that "everybody knows that state laws can't supersede federal laws."[12] But that position, as grounded in reality as it was, did not hold up in the heated atmosphere of generations of southern sensibilities being turned upside down. Political pressure had driven the governor to try every legal loophole to stop desegregation, but a federal court ordered Central High School in Little Rock to desegregate beginning in September of 1957. On August 22, a few days before the first day of school, Georgia Governor Marvin Griffin and Roy Harris, the president of the White Citizens' Councils of Georgia, came to Little Rock at the invitation of the Arkansas White Citizens' Council.

The first White Citizens' Council (WCC) chapter was organized in

Mississippi in July 1954 to resist desegregation after the *Brown v. Board of Education* decision. The movement spread across the Deep South within a few months. Unlike the Ku Klux Klan, the WCC met openly and included many "reputable" community leaders. Their tactics did not involve direct violence but more subtle economic threats to blacks. Members of the WCC were often called "a country club Klan" by outsiders.

Governor Faubus, with some trepidation, invited Governor Griffin and Roy Harris to stay at the governor's mansion. The Georgians' mission was to make sure large crowds at the WCC rallies were wound up sufficiently to vehemently protest integration at Central High. They boasted that Georgia had passed massive resistance laws that had prevented all integration and would continue to do so.[13] At the sight of an angry mob gathering at Central High School on that September morning, Governor Faubus, fearing violence, ordered the Arkansas National Guard to control the crowd outside the school, and the following day Faubus ordered the guard to turn the nine black students away. He cited public safety as his reasons for doing so, claiming white and black students were carrying revolvers. However, segregationists paid little heed to his "apology" regarding safety. The fact that he had defied the federal government made him a hero in their eyes. Faubus learned that his political survival depended upon bending to the wishes of the white majority.

Judge Ronald Davies ruled from the federal bench that Governor Faubus was deliberately defying his court and ordered him to cease and desist.[14] That night Faubus ordered the National Guard troops removed from Central High School grounds and left town for a conference on Sea Island, Georgia.

On September 23, just as Governor Faubus had predicted, a mob surrounded the school. It was impossible for local law enforcement to control the chaotic situation. The police were spread thinly around the school's four-city-block campus and could not cover all the school's entrances where most of the angry protesters congregated. The police escorted the black students out a little-used side entrance before noon to protect their safety.[15] Although sympathizing with the South's position and even agreeing with the idea of states' rights, President Eisenhower could not allow direct defiance of a court order. He federalized the Arkansas National

Guard and ordered a detachment of the 101st Airborne Infantry from Ft. Campbell, Kentucky, to Little Rock.[16]

The black students were the targets of the unmitigated fury of segregationists. These meaner elements of racial prejudice were put on display for the nation. Rocks and vile language rained down on the students. A Mothers League of Central High organized white students to march out of the school in dramatic fashion, and the students then lynched and burned a straw-stuffed dummy of a black student.[17] Most citizens of Little Rock were shocked "as they witnessed a savage rebirth of passion and racial hatred that had lain dormant since Reconstruction days."[18]

The show of boots on the ground by the U.S. Army at Central High School was not a pretty sight flashing across national television either, but the soldiers dispersed the crowd and order was finally restored. Thereafter the Army's mission changed — they were now charged with protecting the black students. In that explosive environment it was surprising that only two black newsmen and one black passerby were beaten, that only twenty-five arrests were made and a scattering of minor instances of violence reported. Hard core segregationists, enraged at seeing federal troops at Central High, cried out in papers and on radio how "the Commie race-mixers are trying to close our schools. 'Federal troops' are occupying the South again."

The rest of the 1957-58 school year, Central High remained desegregated, but the following August, Governor Faubus ordered the three high schools in Little Rock closed. The Women's Emergency Committee to Open Our Schools was formed. The women's group asked for a special election as a way to keep the schools open. The citizens of Little Rock overwhelmingly opposed integration and voted almost three to one in favor of closed schools. More than nine out of ten white students enrolled in other districts or attended private schools. Approximately one-half of black high school students did not attend school during the 1958-59 year.[19]

The voices of bigots made the news while moderate southerners cringed and said little at the sight of racial hatred. The feelings of helplessness and frustration covered Georgia like kudzu vine. Optimism for the future of public schools in the state was at its lowest point. It was within this environment that the Northside mothers in Atlanta were beginning their journey into the unknown.

The month before the Lokey meetings, nine schools were closed in three Virginia counties to stop them from being integrated. Virginia, the seat of the Confederacy, began public discourse against the *Brown* decision soon after the ink was dry on the Supreme Court decision.

James J. Kilpatrick, editor of the *Richard News Leader,* added a significant argument to the anti–*Brown* groundswell in November 1955. Kilpatrick insisted that the *Brown* decision was not an interpretation of the Constitution. "It was an illicit amendment of the document in which 'nine men arrogated unto themselves powers vested by the Constitution in the people' of the states." The *News Leader* argued that given "this rape of the Constitution, does not Virginia have a right and a duty to interpose its sovereignty in a valiant effort to halt the evil?"[20]

This constitutional argument that Kilpatrick preached in speeches and in editorials had a profound effect on lawmakers in the "Confederate" states and many used Kilpatrick's theory as ammunition for total opposition to the enforcement of the *Brown* decision. The logical conclusion to the scenario meant that if states took complete control over their public school enrollment, and thereby refused to comply with *Brown,* the Supreme Court would have to abandon its 1954 decision, just as the country refused to conform to prohibition under the Eighteenth Amendment.[21]

In August and September of 1956 the Virginia General Assembly, with the avid support of Senator Harry F. Byrd, passed legislation that gave the state control of any school in the Commonwealth to which both races had been assigned with the authority to close that school until the governor could reestablish segregation under police powers of the state. The moderate voices in Virginia were silenced by the social elites and the political leadership. The same year, the Georgia Assembly passed a similar resistance bill with one dissenting vote. The bill allowed the governor to subvert any attempts to integrate the schools in any community in the state.

At that time, the *Atlanta Constitution* editor, Ralph McGill, in describing Georgia's state of mind, gave credence to the effects of James Kilpatrick's rhetoric: "There are even now literally thousands of good

Southern people who believe the court's action to be illegal and not applicable to them, because a governor, a congressman, an editor or some other person of position has so said or written."[22]

The Lokeys, the Friedmans and other progressive Atlantans took some comfort in knowing their city had Mayor William Hartsfield at the helm. Although the mayor had no legislative power, he exerted considerable influence from his bully pulpit, promoting the virtues of the city he loved in order to attract big business to turn Atlanta into the modern metropolis he envisioned. He once boasted that he never made a decision without first consulting Coca Cola, the most influential company in town.[23] In office over twenty years, Hartsfield had seen the city evolve from a large genteel town to the big city it was becoming by the mid-fifties. The mayor boasted that Atlanta's airport would eventually be bigger and busier than that in Los Angeles or Chicago.

When the racial crisis began to heat up after the 1954 Supreme Court decision, Hartsfield asked Governor Marvin Griffin to allow Atlanta to hold a referendum on whether to close its schools in case they were forced to desegregate. Griffin's refusal to budge from his total segregation policy enraged Hartsfield: "I don't give a damn what Griffin or anyone else said, I refuse to let Georgia go through another period of ignorance."[24]

Hartsfield had come into office as a segregationist, but his interest in expanding the city's economy and his understanding of the rising importance of the black vote relegated his support of white supremacy to the background. In 1957, the black urban vote saved the mayor from defeat in the primary election when a large majority of whites voted for his opponent, the rabid segregationist Lester Maddox. Maddox had accused Hartsfield of being a pawn of the NAACP.[25] Hartsfield countered by defining himself as protector of the social order, reminding the voters that Atlantans are proud of the way the two races live side by side. He told them, "We do not want the hatred and bitterness of Montgomery and Little Rock."[26] Hartsfield did not need the black vote to win the general election because many white voters had been turned off by Maddox's extreme positions, which prompted the reelected mayor to claim that victory proved that the people of Atlanta did not want the progress and growth of the city marred by racial strife. Hartsfield, forever the pragmatist, solidified his position on racial moderation, which pleased Atlanta's progressive element and infuriated the die-hard segregationists.

Hartsfield cringed at the prospect of a closed public school system in his beloved city. "It will do little good to bring about more brick, stone and concrete while a shocked and amazed world looks at a hundred thousand innocent children roaming the streets."[27]

In fact, William B. Hartsfield, who was born on Butler Street in Atlanta in 1890, probably knew the history of the city by heart. Not that he dwelled in the past. To the contrary, he lived, planned and worked with a vivid future in mind. As Atlanta found itself at the crossroads of the impending fight over school desegregation, the mayor must have vowed to himself: This time the battle of Atlanta will not end in defeat.

Chapter 2

A City Too Busy to Hate

To make a trip to Atlanta was like going to Moscow or Beijing. It was a totally different world.[1]

— Jimmy Carter,
former President of the United States

Throughout its history, Atlanta has had outstanding leaders who believed in the city's future like William Hartsfield. In 1879, Henry W. Grady, an avid promoter of Atlanta's virtues as a progressive journalist and businessman (he owned the *Atlanta Constitution*), tried to reconcile the North and South in his editorials and public addresses. He believed in putting aside old grievances and working toward a "new South." Grady wanted to see the region diversify its crops and industries and modernize with the help of Northern capital. On a trip Grady made to New York City in 1886, reporters asked him what he was planning to say in a speech to the New England Society of New York where he was to be the first Southerner to ever speak before the group. The gentleman from Georgia replied with characteristic humor: "The Lord only knows. I have thought of a thousand things to say, five hundred of which if I say they will murder me when I get back home, and the other five hundred of which will get me murdered at the banquet."[2] He knew his role was not to bemoan the South's defeat, but rather, to show himself as a peacemaker and promoter for his beloved city and state. Southerners "have smoothed the path southward, wiped out the place where Mason and Dixon's line used to be, and hung out our latchstring to you and yours," he told his audience. [3]

Although his legacy of trying to modernize his city lives on, Grady remained an arch segregationist with a firm belief in white supremacy. The inequality of the races, he wrote, "is instinctive-deeper than prejudice or pride, and bred in the bone and blood."[4]

Despite beginning small, burning to the ground and faltering through setbacks, Atlanta was envisioned by many of its great leaders to be bigger and better. Atlanta's roots hold the key to how the city not only survived, but flourished to become the "Jewel of the South."

* * *

A Cherokee Indian trail, which is now Peachtree Street in Atlanta, ran along the ridge to a trading post, "The Standing Peachtree," on the banks of the Chattahoochee River, seven miles from present-day Five Points. During the 1830s, Methodist circuit riders blazed trails through the area and when campgrounds were established near Sandy Springs and Lawrenceville, connecting trails were widened into wagon routes.[5]

Plans were made in 1836 for a state railroad to be built through the mountains of north Georgia with the southern terminus to be in this area. Railroads in the lower part of the state planned to extend their lines to connect with the northern routes. A stake was driven at the junction of these tracks, at a point that is within present-day Atlanta. When the state legislature chartered the town of "Marthasville" in 1843 (in honor of the daughter of ex–Governor Wilson Lumpkin who had furthered the state's interest in railroads), there were two stores, the Western & Atlantic Railroad office, a hotel and about a dozen dwellings.[6]

Two years later, a lively trading center was beginning to emerge because of booming cotton commerce and heavy railroad traffic that brought in lumberjacks, wood haulers, railroad workers, and more merchants to serve the growing population. Business leaders eventually came to believe that "Marthasville" did not aptly describe the bustling railroad center they envisioned, and the chief engineer of the Georgia Railroad suggested the name, Atlanta, "the terminus of the Western & Atlantic Railroad — masculine Atlantic, feminine Atlanta."[7]

Churches and decent citizens kept the pressure on to clean up the rough town of saloons, brothels, gambling houses, street fights and murders. Gradually, business and political leaders merged their work ethic with their Protestant morality to bring law and order to Atlanta. The Christian temperance movement gained enough support to outlaw alcohol at times, locking horns with the more free-spirited city dwellers.

The twin pillars of Atlanta society-business and religion — continued to be dominant influences throughout the city's history and during the school desegregation crisis. The commerce sector, which traditionally aligned with politicians, remained wedded to the status quo, refusing to help the open-school movement during its early stages. Ultimately, however, under pressure from the mayor and open-school advocates, businessmen realized their interests were better served by keeping schools open. Atlanta's religious leaders, at first reluctant to lead in what many Christians believed was a moral struggle, became a voice for open schools by the end of 1958.

By 1861, Atlanta could boast several fine hotels, a courthouse, churches, and a commercial district with brick buildings, which were most prominent on Whitehall Street. Atlanta was an upcountry town without the planters' influence, and boasted a population of some 9,500. In coastal towns, such as Savannah and Charleston, slave populations ranged as high as 40 percent of the total population, but in Atlanta slaves were only 20 percent of the total population. However, slave markets were nevertheless located next to the railroad depot with signs that read: SLAVE AUCTION ROOMS, SLAVES BOUGHT AND SOLD HERE.[8]

When the Civil War broke out and President Lincoln blockaded the southern states, optimism still ran high in Atlanta. City leaders boasted that the war would be over in a matter of months, and the Confederacy would punish the Unionists once and for all. The populace was told that Atlanta's Mechanic Fire Company No. 2, which headed the home guard unit, "is a sufficient guarantee ... in protecting and defending, if need be, the lives and property of the good people of Atlanta."[9]

The voices boasting of a quick victory gave way to harsh reality by the summer of 1864. Federal and Confederate troops battled outside the city — Atlanta was under siege. On September 2, with explosions lighting up the sky, Atlanta's Mayor Calhoun rode with a few citizens three miles out Marietta Street to the Federal lines and surrendered the city.[10] Except for the few who sympathized with the Unionists, most of the people began their flight from occupied Atlanta. General Sherman's troops set torches to the wooden buildings and blew up the more substantial structures with gunpowder on November 14. The railroad tracks had already been demolished. A Federal officer wrote his wife: "All the pictures and verbal descriptions of hell I have ever seen never gave me half so vivid an idea of it as did this flame-wrapped city tonight. Gate City of the South, farewell."[11]

As General Sherman finally arrived in Atlanta on September 7, a black man, suddenly a free man, said "Lord, massa, is dat General Sherman? I'se glad I'se seen him. I just wanted to see de man what made old massa run."[12]

General Sherman's march through Georgia to Savannah left the land that had supported a prospering cotton economy in ruin, but if the land had remained fertile, there were no railroads to transport crops to market. Because livestock and crops were confiscated from the wealthy and poorer plantations alike, the population was nearly starving, which marked the beginning of the unraveling of Georgia's plantation society.

Many freed slaves left the South, but others remained to claim land for their own farms. In fact, great numbers stayed on to change their slave status to tenant farmer under white ownership, and others moved to Atlanta to find work and safety from white violence. "Darktown" or "Shermantown," as whites referred to the settlement in the east end of Atlanta along present-day Decatur Street and Auburn Avenue, grew in population and so did the opportunities for those who lived there. Thirty years after the Civil War, there were black druggists, grocers, undertakers, educators and preachers who had become the colored aristocracy. These mostly light-skinned blacks lived in brick houses along tree-lined streets and built their lives around their churches, social clubs and black colleges. Atlanta's white and black communities lived in parallel worlds, knowing virtually nothing about each other.

The Reconstruction Acts required Georgia to hold a constitutional convention in December 1867, but in Milledgeville, the state capital, hotels and boarding houses refused to accommodate black delegates of the Republican party.[13] The party got its revenge by moving the state capital to Atlanta with the help of city leaders, who promised to build any state government building required for ten years.[14] Moving the capital to Atlanta embittered rural politicians and much of the population south of the city as expressed in *The Southern Recorder:* "The people are not such a set of asses as to listen to such an idea. Atlanta may have the penitentiary if she wants it; as it is an institution that will not come amiss to many of her population."[15] Atlanta gained more status as the legislative and judicial center, but its focus remained commercial.

The 1867 convention mandated by the Reconstruction Acts required Georgia to write black suffrage into its state constitution, to elect a state government based on the new constitution and to ratify the Fourteenth Amendment — all to be accomplished under watchful eyes of Yankee officers. After the state met these requirements, Georgia would be readmitted to the Union. Many of these laws in the war's aftermath were passed over President Johnson's veto.

Northerners coming into town as representatives of the Freedman's Bureau, a Reconstruction program, soon became known as carpetbaggers, who along with local opportunists (called scalawags) were seen by most conservative Democrats and their followers as dominating the state's Republican party. But history tells us that these "radicals" tried to set Georgia on a more progressive course, in line with the free labor practices of the North, and they also tried to bring in northern capital to the state in an effort to diversify the cotton economy. They also courted blacks to run for office and supported education reform for both races.

White Georgians were humiliated by their defeat in the Civil War, and now they were faced with accepting changes in their society that they believed to be outrageous. The members of the northern reform movement mistakenly believed that they could quickly change the state from an agrarian paternalistic society into an industrialized model. The North might as well have asked white Georgians to invite General Sherman to dinner along with their former slaves. The deep resentment from this period, festering for generations, created a legacy that is littered with missed opportunities for economic progress and enlightenment.

Widespread corruption in the capital city under the Republicans added more fuel to the struggle for political power between the Democrats who led the resistance to change and the Republicans who supported the federal plan for Reconstruction. However, funds from Washington that were earmarked to help local citizens recover after the war ended up in the pockets of men in power. Newspapers reported lavish meals and entertainment offered to businessmen who were being courted to bring capital to rebuild the city.

By 1871, some of that outside capital had gone toward the construction of 400 residential and commercial buildings. Mercantile and industrial operations (rolling mills, brick factories, iron foundries) expanded, and a street railway on Whitehall Street began operating from Five Points to the West End. The busy railroads made Atlanta the distribution center for canned meat and flour from the Midwest, grain from Tennessee, Kentucky and the upper Mississippi valley and guano from Peru. The vision of Atlanta's pioneer railroad barons was coming true. The city liked to boast that it had or would soon have all the modern conveniences. A northern visitor reported in 1878 that Atlanta had artificial ice and a Turkish bath. The next year brought the installation of the first telephone exchange.

Democrats led by white supremacist plantation owners and their allies began to defeat the Republicans after 1871, labeling Reconstruction a "crime." Atlanta business leaders were more interested in moving forward, than licking wounds of the past. General Sherman, also ready to mend fences, arrived in Atlanta in 1879 and was asked by a young reporter from the *Constitution* why the general had burned the city down fifteen years earlier. The general held the reporter's hand. "Young man, when I got to Atlanta, what was left of the Confederacy could roughly be compared to your hand. Atlanta was the palm and by destroying it I spared myself much further fighting." But he added that the same reasons he cited for burning Atlanta would make it a great city one day.[16]

The twentieth century ushered in an ambitious public relations campaign to attract more business to Atlanta. Brochures displayed the advantages of living in an up-and-coming southern city — a moderate climate, miles of street car lines, gas and electric lights, tree-lined residential areas, swank hotels, theater and opera and skyscrapers.[17] Black people, who now constituted 43 percent of the population, were not part of this slick advertising campaign extolling the virtues of the modern city, however. There was little to brag about in "colored town" where the majority of poor blacks, whose jobs in white homes earned meager wages, lived in shanties.

Northerners, too, were on the bandwagon of progress for the new century calling on white supremacists to silence the race question in politics. The popular sentiment declared that racism hindered the nation's progress, but at the same time the old pro-abolitionist journal, the *Atlantic Monthly*, published articles on the "universal supremacy of the Anglo-Saxon," and the last black Congressman was sent home to North Carolina in the spring of 1901.[18]

Racial conflict in Atlanta reflected the national mood after a heated gubernatorial race in 1906. Both candidates, Atlantans Hoke Smith and Clark Howell, tried to outdo each other in running on a white supremacy platform and promoting "the legal disenfranchisement of the 223,000 male negroes of voting age in Georgia."[19] In September, newspaper boys shouted from street corners with papers held high, "Extra! Third Assault on White Women by a Negro Brute," "Extra! Bold Negro Kisses White Girl's Hand."[20] The climate was ripe for an explosion. Throngs of white men ran down the streets of Atlanta with clubs and makeshift weapons attacking and beating blacks to death. After three days of rioting and with nearly 50 blacks dead, the state militia restored order to a shocked and frightened city.[21] The terror of white hatred left deep scars in the black community. White Atlantans' fear of a mob gone wild burned in the collective memory and there was one Atlanta teenager at the time, William Hartsfield, who must never have forgotten the disastrous consequences of racial strife in the city he loved.

In 1900, the white supremacist mentality of the day dictated that its Atlanta promoters dare not mention the highly successful Morris Brown College for blacks, which had been founded by the American Missionary Association two years after the Civil War ended and eventually developed into a five-college complex. This academic stronghold was largely unknown to white Atlanta before and during the public school crisis. The segregation of whites and blacks in housing and public facilities, including schools, made it inevitable that whites would only know blacks as cooks, maids, and yardmen employed in their homes.

After fighting off Reconstruction policies, plantation owners and their allies returned to running their own fiefdoms with little intrusion from outsiders. Atlanta represented everything rural folks disliked — fast-paced living, all sorts of foreigners moving into the area and the institutions of higher learning, which they suspected promoted ideas that did not fit the Georgia way of life. The plantation culture's interests and those of big business coincided on major issues such as low taxes, keeping labor costs down and maintaining the southern way of life. Consequently, with the financial backing of business and agriculture, small-county politicians were elected to the state assembly to block progressive legislation. Therefore, with a meager tax base and with education remaining a low priority, the state did not support public schools in any significant way until the mid–1940s. The one-party legislature was dominated by votes from small rural counties, which made it easier to pass the stringent resistance laws against school desegregation in the 1950s. The two-party system did not rise again in Georgia in any meaningful way until the 1960s.

Chapter 3

Who's Running Georgia?

Attorney Gen. Eugene Cook Tuesday charged the NAACP is more "un–American than the Communist Party."[1]

— Atlanta Constitution

By the third meeting in the Lokeys' living room, even the kitchen chairs were in use. Fran Breeden came that Wednesday night on crutches, thinking she would not know anyone in the room. Fran and her family had recently moved to Atlanta, but she was not the least bit shy about facing a room of new people. She and her husband, Tom, had moved their family so many times that introducing herself came naturally. Her energy and personality drove her to get involved wherever they lived; she had been active in the PTA, Scouts, church, Junior League, and the League of Women Voters. Although her family could afford private schools, Fran believed in public schools and made sure her children were enrolled in them.

Fran had read Harold Martin's column in Sunday's *Atlanta Journal-Constitution* while recuperating in the hospital from foot surgery. She was stunned at Martin's low-key plea to Atlantans to wake up if they wanted their schools to survive. With four school-age children, alarm bells sounded in Fran's head. She phoned the *Journal* office and asked for Harold Martin. She told him his column had triggered her fear for the first time that schools might actually close, and she asked what could she do? Martin suggested she call his brother-in-law Ham Lokey. He said there was a small group getting together to discuss the crisis.

But it turned out Fran had seen Muriel and Maxine at parents' meetings for an experimental program for gifted seventh graders. All three of the women's oldest children had been selected for the class at Garden Hills Elementary School. It was an exciting new venture that would challenge students with advanced work.

Fran, who was pretty and slender, moved with ease into new situations. She settled into a chair with her bandaged foot propped on a hassock while Muriel introduced her to the others. Fran could not have realized then how much her actor training at the New School in New York would be put to use in the ensuing months.

One of the few men in the room, Harry Boyte, had been speaking when Fran entered. He sat rigidly in one of the straight-back chairs because of a chronic back problem. This was Boyte's first time at the Lokey's residence. He was an outspoken liberal who headed the local Human Relations Council, a small group of whites and blacks dedicated to improving race relations in the city.

Boyte admonished the group to take the moral high ground in this crisis and speak out for the NAACP's court case. He felt there was a bigger issue here than just keeping the schools open for white children.

Maxine Friedman expressed a different point of view. She said this was about mothers who weren't going to stand for their children not having schools to attend. She did not think it was their job to take sides on this hot political issue, and she urged everyone to stay focused on the one goal of keeping schools open.

Boyte answered that the group would be missing the most important point of this struggle if they failed to take a public stand on the rightness of the NAACP suit against segregated schools.

At these early meetings most women and the few men who attended had not formed opinions about the NAACP suit per se. Their meetings were all about what they could do to keep the schools open. Maxine Friedman kept her eye on that ball throughout the crisis.

Fran Breeden, seeing that no agreement could be reached on this divisive topic, suggested that they concentrate on seeing how they could spread the truth of what was actually at stake.

Ham Lokey had been uncharacteristically quiet until he reminded the group that most people believed the schools would not actually close. They believed what the politicians kept telling them, which is what they wanted to hear: If the federal court rules against the board of education, the state would just run private schools instead.

Some of the women questioned if it was even possible for the state to run private schools. Lokey thought that it was not likely because there were too many legal problems with private school funding laws. The way it stood now, he added, if (and he thought more likely it was when) the courts ruled that Atlanta schools had to desegregate, state law would close every schoolhouse in the state.

Someone active with the League of Women Voters echoed Ham Lokey's political insight with the suggestion that they must inform the public so they would put pressure on their legislators to change the resistance laws. She said they had to get Frances Pauley, the former state League president, on board because she knew the "capitol boys" like no one else.

Boyte resoundingly agreed with bringing Pauley on board. He knew she was a fighter from their joint participation in liberal causes. But Pauley had made a vow that she would never again join an all-white group, and so declined to participate during those first months.

By the next meeting Muriel had to limit the number of people invited. The word had spread, and the group now realized it was time to move out of the Lokeys' living room to a public space.

Maxine booked a public meeting for November 18 at a Jewish community hall. Two days before the scheduled meeting, however, the staff of the hall canceled the event. The subject was too controversial. In mid–October there had been a bomb blast at the Atlanta synagogue, causing $96,000 in damage, which made the staff quite wary of the danger.

The women had to scramble to find another public space and came up with the Spring Street Elementary School. The P.T.A. agreed to make the school crisis the subject of their meeting on the 18th. To change the meeting place, the group set up a telephone tree and managed to bring out nearly 400 people, mostly women, to hear state legislator Muggsy Smith, who represented Fulton County. It was the first public meeting ever held on the school crisis. Smith gave an impassioned speech and put his reputation on the line. He was committing political suicide.

"What I have to say tonight concerns our beloved public schools, yes, *this school*, where my wife teaches and my children attend.... We too long have sat idly by in the hopes that some Moses shall lead us out of the morass of a situation that is not of our own choosing, and for which no remedy has been found.... Even those leaders who originated the private school plan now doubt its efficacy. Decisions in other states have proven their inadequacy. How much longer, then, shall we depend upon them? Shall it be after our schools are closed?"[2]

A man sitting in the front row announced in a booming voice, "You can't keep the schools open with what you're saying." He got up and walked out of the meeting while loud murmurs of disapproval rippled through the audience.

Smith did not skip a beat. He continued his speech, describing what it would be like if the schools closed — cobwebs throughout the buildings, mice running through the halls, weeds overtaking once-mowed green lawns, children underfoot all day long or maybe so bored that they're out on the streets.

"What of Georgia's economic future?" he asked. "Does anyone think that a large industry will move to a place where its employees cannot send their children to school?"[3]

"With this disheartening picture in mind, I would like to speak beyond the confines of this meeting. Yes, even beyond the city limits, for what I have to say I want to say to all the people of Georgia...."[4]

He spoke as urgently as a Methodist preacher at a revival meeting.

"Yes, hear my words. For as surely as the sun did set this afternoon and shall surely rise (God willing) tomorrow morning, so shall your schools be closed when those in Atlanta are closed.... This is not a City-County fight.... This is one time that all of us should join together in an effort to avoid the inevitable results of the closing of our public schools."[5]

Smith went on to describe what a private high school in Little Rock looked like:

"The school's in an old orphanage building. They have no chemistry laboratory, no foreign languages, no sports or extra-curricular activities, and no cafeteria. And all teachers are from retired rolls, since no current teacher can break her contract with the state to teach in a private school."[6]

Muriel and Maxine sat in the audience, their hearts racing. They knew time was running out. They had to act now.

Smith urged those assembled to take the stickers he brought, WE WANT PUBLIC SCHOOLS, to put them on their cars and anywhere else they could think of to show their support. He also encouraged them to talk with others about what this crisis really meant. He pleaded with the audience in closing:

"If we the people do not rise to this great challenge, and that immediately, then in a few months we shall come to this building and see through tear-dimmed eyes, the sign:

FOR SALE — SPRING STREET SCHOOL."[7]

Maxine went home with admiration in her heart for Representative Smith. He had guts and that was a rare quality in politicians.[8]

Senator Richard Russell spoke to the school crisis in December following the Spring Street School meeting, declaring that private schools are a last resort. He refuted the claim that businesses were being scared off from coming to the state, despite the arguments of integrationists that "the threat to our system of public education has terrified every businessman who is thinking of locating in the state."[9]

Muggsy Smith and a few other representatives from metropolitan Atlanta had no real voice in the state assembly for good reason. Senators Russell and Talmadge, beholden to their "outside Atlanta" constituents, worked in unison with the majority serving in the General Assembly. The current school desegregation crisis made it abundantly clear who ran Georgia. It was not Atlanta. Herein lay the crux of the problem.

The rest of Georgia, with more land than people, dictated what would and would not happen in the state. To grasp why the city, a center for colleges and universities, with a thriving commerce and an expanding population, could not override courthouse politics, one must look at Georgia's foundations, its long-held pride and prejudices. It was the embedded prejudices within the system itself that held the state back in education, in industrial progress, and in modernizing social welfare and labor practices.

The South's most revered hero, Robert E. Lee, knew the sting of defeat better than anyone, but after surrendering at Appomattox, he said that the major aim of every Southerner should be to unite in "the allayment of passion, the dissipation of prejudice and restoration of reason."[10] It is a Lee legacy unknown to the majority of Georgia politicians in 1958, whose passions overwhelmed their reason.

* * *

Under General James E. Oglethorpe, the English established a colony west of Carolina along the Savannah River in 1733 as a utopian sanctuary for England's downtrodden poor. Only the "worthy poor" passed the screening process for free passage to Georgia, 50 acres of free land, and a year's rations. Laws in the new colony banned slavery, hard alcohol, blacks, Roman Catholics, liquor dealers, and lawyers.

Olgethorpe envisioned a town-oriented society of tradesmen and small farmers. He had no interest in replicating the single-crop slave labor economies, such as the sugar colonies of the British West Indies or rice-growing areas of South Carolina or tobacco-producing Virginia. The idea was to produce raw silk from mulberry trees, grow grapevines for wine export, olive trees for their oil, and dyes and drugs from native plants. But these crops never materialized sufficiently to pay for goods that the colony needed from abroad. Georgia planters were not getting prosperous, while their Carolina neighbors thrived in a slave-labor rice plantation economy. The debate over slavery rocked the colony for a decade. Seventeen years after Georgia was settled, the slavery prohibition was lifted, and by the time of the American Revolution, slaves composed nearly one-half of the state's population. So much for the original idealism of a utopian community.

After Eli Whitney perfected the cotton gin in 1793, cotton became profitable. Georgia planters were no longer the "poor cousins" of their Carolina neighbors. Soon Georgia produced more cotton than anywhere else in the world. Despite Olgethorpe's efforts, few wore Georgia silk. Millions were to wear Georgia cotton, however. Cotton was king, even for the small white farmer who also owned slaves, but the greatest wealth was concentrated in huge plantations across the state. In 1860 at least half of the total wealth of the state was held in slave property. Georgia's industrial development lagged far behind that of the rest of the nation and was confined to gristmills that produced flour and meal and sawmills for lumber.

The interests of cotton planters and Atlanta's railroad barons converged sufficiently to make both successful before the Civil War. Railroads moved the cotton to far-flung markets and everybody got rich. But in the years following the destruction of Atlanta and much of the state, the infusion of northern capital into Atlanta moved the city toward a more diversified economy. Atlanta also had a more diverse population compared to the rest of the state—making the city a beacon of hope for young men and women escaping from poverty. However, it was also an emerging battleground for the fight between contrasting interests of country and city.

As the South moved closer to secession from the Union in 1861, a Georgia planter expressed the prevailing sentiment at the time: "In this country have arisen two races which, although claiming a common parentage, have been entirely separated by climate, by morals, by religion—that they cannot coexist under the same government."[11]

Ending the war in defeat only intensified the will to hold onto the way of life that had characterized the Old South. Congress launched three Reconstruction programs in Georgia before the contentious state passed requirements for rejoining the Union in July 1870. The Reconstruction period brought about the creation of the Ku Klux Klan, a brotherhood of property owners who feared losing their rights and their land to emancipated slaves as well as their entire plantation system to a new order imposed on them by the North. To the planter, the Republican party became synonymous with Yankee carpetbaggers and local scalawags who had taken control of the Negro vote, and synonymous with those whose aim was to impose radical changes to the society. The Democrats preached that they were the saviors of the South from radical Republicanism. They were hell-bent on preserving as much of the Old South as possible by any means they deemed necessary, even if it required Ku Klux Klan terror.

The Democrats were successful in making sure state politics were run from the county courthouse for the next hundred years by establishing the county unit system of elections in 1917.

All 159 counties were classified into three categories by population: eight urban counties, 30 town counties and 121 rural counties. The number of unit votes each county received in statewide primaries was based upon this classification. The combined unit votes from town and rural counties outnumbered the urban unit votes by large margins. Although the rural/town counties accounted for only 32 percent of the state population in 1960, they controlled 59 percent of the total unit vote.[12]

Without a viable two-party system in the state, the candidate who won the Democratic primary in the summer won the election. Although in some cases a run-off was required between two Democratic candidates, the fall election became mostly a formality.

With only a hiccup in Georgia politics during the Populist era (a late-nineteenth-century reform movement against white supremacy and the one-party system), the Old South plantation culture held its grip on the state by disenfranchising those in more populous areas, those who held progressive ideas. The county unit system reduced the pool of voters to a number that was easily influenced and manipulated. The system could not work without corporate money backing the statewide political machines and leaders in small, under populated counties. Corporations financed the candidate of their choice—the one who would look with favor on their interests in the legislature. The common rationale for the system perpetuated by farmers was as follows: "We'd have no voice in state government without it." And underlying all the political talk raged the cultural war between country folks and residents of Atlanta, the city deemed "the root of all evil"[13] by outsiders. Rural Georgians ran the political show while resentment from urban voters grew.

The old resentment against outside agitators and their values, which had been propelled through the generations since Reconstruction, was the fuse that set off the emotional fire of stump speeches on the steps of county courthouses across the state. The granddaddy of them all, Eugene Talmadge, preached against New Deal programs when Georgia's economy hit rock bottom during the Depression. Talmadge's fear of federal government encroachment on state authority outweighed everything. He advocated relinquishing no power whatsoever—his own, especially. He ranted at rallies that communities with the help of neighbors and churches, could take care of themselves. "The wild man from Sugar Creek" loved to tell his followers: "The poor dirt farmer ain't got but three friends on this earth: God Almighty, Sears Roebuck, and Gene Talmadge."[14] And the people believed him.

Governor Talmadge boasted he never campaigned in a county with a streetcar. He often told his courthouse cronies: "Come see me at the mansion. We'll sit on the front porch and piss over the rail on those city bastards."[15]

In 1936, Georgia elected Eurith (Ed) D. Rivers, a moderate, who answered the voters' plea for help by welcoming New Deal programs, saving the state from economic collapse. Finally, Georgia swallowed its outdated pride and gladly received help from "outsiders." President Roosevelt depicted the South in 1938 as "the Nation's Number 1 Economic Problem." Cotton was taking its last breath on the landscape and farm foreclosures were commonplace — whites and blacks alike were out of work and dirt poor.

Gene Talmadge engineered an all-out assault on President Roosevelt and the New Deal in his run to unseat Georgia's junior senator, Richard B. Russell, in 1936. His attacks backfired. Senator Russell defended the president and his program and cruised to a solid victory.

Consequently, Talmadge decided to tone down his fiery rhetoric during the 1940 governors race, but his hatred of Roosevelt and the New Deal and his hostility to new ideas and cultural change had not changed one iota. To Talmadge and his followers, Ed Rivers had courted ultraliberals in Georgia, giving them a toehold in state politics. One Talmadge advocate explained: "Their [liberals'] objectives varied as to purpose. Some were bent upon ending the segregation of the black and white races in the South; others worked for the abolition of the county unit system; and others agitated for repeal of the poll tax." One of the emerging strongholds for these ultraliberals seemed to be the state university system.

Soon after his inauguration in 1941, Talmadge unleashed an attack on "foreign professors trying to destroy the sacred traditions of the South," some of whom were not only educated in "foreign" universities in the Midwest and elsewhere but were identified with the Rosenwald Fund, or as Talmadge phrased it, "were receiving Jew money for niggers."[16] The governor, an ex officio member of the Board of Regents, led the move to fire the president of the teachers college at Statesboro, the dean of the University of Georgia college of education, and eight other university system employees. He wanted to fire all educators who were not Georgians, but he gave up the idea as an impossible goal when he learned there were seven hundred non–Georgian educators in the system. Nevertheless, he sanctioned committees to find "subversive" material in textbooks and university system libraries. In response to all these measures, the Southern Association of Colleges and Secondary Schools and other accreditation organizations dropped Georgia's ten state-supported colleges for whites.

World War II began, engendering an economic boom in the state. Factories multiplied and all able-bodied men were either in the armed services or working. And for the first time women in the larger towns and cities were holding down jobs outside the home. The state was taking the first steps toward social change.

Ellis Arnall, the state attorney general and ally of former governor Rivers, made academic freedom his central issue when he ran against Talmadge in 1942. The Atlanta papers fumed in their editorials, declaring, "Talmadge's candidacy is an insult to Georgia's intelligence." Talmadge's attack on the University of Georgia, beloved by Georgians across the state, galvanized conservatives and liberals alike to show their strong opposition to his attempts at dismantling the state's university system.

Arnall became an able and innovative governor, providing a brief respite from courthouse politics. He emphasized economic development, including the organization of labor unions, believing that poverty lay at the base of Georgia's problems. There was a strong movement afoot to push Georgia into the 20th century: to reform an archaic and undemocratic political one-party system, to use more tax dollars to upgrade pathetically deficient schools, and to modernize roads and other public works. The state constitution was amended to four-year terms for governor, which allowed Arnall to stay in office until 1946.

The Supreme Court's ruling in 1944 (*Smith v. Allwright*) outlawed the white Democratic primary and was hailed as a giant step toward reform of Georgia's political system.[17] Two years later, a federal district court opened the Georgia primary to black voters. The white primary had been the bulwark of the old order since 1900: white supremacy and black disenfranchisement.

The real threat of large numbers of blacks and white liberals voting out the "old guard" stirred Gene Talmadge and his cohorts, who were never known for fair and temperate races anyway, to achieve a new low in 1946. The Talmadge "wool hat" boys ran the dirtiest campaign Georgia had ever witnessed. It was his last and most desperate race. This time the old strategy came laced with an insidious underbelly: Concentrate on a sufficient number of small rural counties to win a majority of county unit votes, and in the process effectively disenfranchise black voters. Talmadge headquarters sent tens of thousands of registration challenge forms to supporters in these rural counties, advising "if the good white people will explain it to the Negroes around over the state just right I don't think they will want to vote."[18] Talmadge knew the poor white farmers, who were largely uneducated, had the most to lose from blacks voting. He played to their racist fears and prejudices, flattering them by suggesting they were higher on the social scale than the lowly "Negra." A Talmadge speech line that said "a Negra should come to my back door with hat in hand"[19] perpetuated his appeal to rural whites. There was a huge turnout of voters in the 1946 gubernatorial election, resulting in Roy Carmichael winning the popular vote and Talmadge taking the county unit vote, which was the only one that counted.

Lillian Smith, noted author and the leading liberal voice in Georgia at the time, wrote in 1943, "A rich white made a bargain with a poor white: 'you boss the nigger, and I'll boss the money.' The rich man explained that at the time, because of limited capital available in the South, high profits required low wages, but 'remember you're a sight better off and better than the black man. And remember there's nothing so good for folks to do than go to church on Sundays.'"[20] The plantation culture avoided class struggle by including poor whites into the common brotherhood of white men. The bargain rested on poor whites not taking part in any labor strife and continuing to vote for the old guard politicians. Their payoff was that they were free to lynch and flog, to burn and threaten without fear from the law.

The bargain was invented by men like Talmadge. He offered rural Georgians the "sinister brew" of racism, a false populist platform (a fight for the "little man"), and the Old South economic system. Large-scale intimidation of potential black voters was in full force across rural Georgia. Blacks were warned: "You'd better not try to register to vote. Or else."

Blacks who registered to vote would be fired, denied credit at the white man's store, and live under constant threat of violence. Houses burned in the middle of the night, lynchings still happened, and harassment and threats to men and women were commonplace.

One hundred thousand black Georgians registered and voted against Talmadge in that infamous 1946 race despite of such tactics, most of whom resided in Atlanta and other more densely populated counties. But the Talmadge strategy worked. The rural counties came through again for the racist demagogue. Paternalistic plantation politics still reigned in Georgia eighty years after Reconstruction.

Herman Talmadge, Eugene's son, was elected governor in a special election in 1948 after bizarre and duplicitous maneuvering to seize the post after his father died before he could be sworn in as governor. Moderates in the state recoiled at another Talmadge running Georgia.

Indeed, the son had learned demagogic politics at his father's knee, and he was savvy enough to amend the old line with the new mantra of southern politics: liberals equal communists equals the mongrelization of the races. The young Talmadge could now use the communist threat as the biggest possible version of an outside agitator attempting to destroy Georgia's traditions. After all, communist propaganda preached equality for all, organized labor, and equal distribution of wealth. Herman Talmadge deftly used the real fear of what such a disastrous system could do to free enterprise and to southern society's values. Conservative business leaders with the help of like-minded politicians defeated the labor movement's efforts to organize in Georgia and other southern states, largely because of such false associations with communism.

Herman Talmadge quickly became the South's foremost spokesman for the defenders of white supremacy. He and other state officials constantly condemned the communists, the federal courts, and the NAACP, whom they deemed outside meddlers seeking to disrupt Georgia's harmonious race relations. Herman Talmadge declared with the arrogant flair of a con artist, "The races will not be mixed come hell or high water."

Governor Herman Talmadge was smart enough, however, to balance the old order with urban and industrial progress and racial traditionalism. But despite Talmadge's influences, black voter registrations increased (concentrated in Atlanta and smaller cities), and black educators won election to school boards in Augusta and Atlanta during the early 1950s. The old bargain between the rich and the poor white as adversaries against the black man was breaking apart.

The Talmadge forces responded to the federal courts' insistence that if schools were separate they must be equal by championing the Minimum Foundation Program on the floor of the legislature. The bill passed in 1949, promising a minimum level of school funding for all Georgia students, but the law meant little until it was adequately funded.

Expenditures on schools had increased during the prosperous post–World War II years, but Georgia still had a hodgepodge system of common schools, ranging from a relatively adequate education for white children in affluent urban areas to underpaid one-teacher rural schools struggling to educate youngsters, most of whom were black. In 1951, Talmadge pushed through a three percent sales tax that dramatically increased state income and provided funding for the Minimum Foundation Program. For the first time, Georgia established a public school system, which is recognized as the most modernizing reforms of the era. Soon afterward with a spyglass on the future, Georgia legislators put a constitutional amendment before the voters in 1954 permitting the abandonment of public education in the event of forced desegregation. The League of Women Voters and other concerned citizens vigorously opposed the amendment and worked to defeat it, but despite their heroic efforts, the amendment was narrowly ratified.

Herman Talmadge prepared for the battle ahead by building schools for Negroes and providing them with new books and up-to-date equipment. He concentrated on rural areas where the paternalistic plantation culture still existed. Talmadge reasoned that with good schools run by black educators, they would opt for segregated schools for their people rather than take a chance on having to share their turf with whites. In 1955, the Talmadge administration published a thick booklet entitled *Schoolhouse Story,* which included photographs of white schools being built to replace old ones. The last four pages were devoted to black schools, describing the improved facilities as better than ever.[21]

With all the ranting and raving that filled the air from Georgia politicians about protecting segregation, it would seem the state was still shack-led to Reconstruction carpetbaggers. In reality, their days were numbered. Conservatives from rural and small-town Georgia were losing ground due to the rise of suburbia and the growing influence of Atlanta's corporate and business interests. The state's economic and political structure was being reshaped.

Nevertheless, the Talmadge machine clung to the results of polls that showed most Georgians were segregationists, justifying their obsession to defend white supremacy.

The League of Women Voters and other concerned citizens, espe-cially in Atlanta, worked for years to overturn the county unit system. Morris Abram, a highly respected and well-known Atlanta lawyer from Fitzgerald, Georgia, argued before the United States Supreme Court against the disproportionate value accorded to votes as determined by citizens' place of residence (*Sanders v. Gray*). The high court ruled in favor of Abram's argument on March 18, 1963, citing the disproportionate value of votes constituted a violation of the Fourteenth Amendment to the United States Constitution. Abram and his allies had been fighting for "one-man, one-vote" in state and district courts since 1952. The system running Georgia since the end of Reconstruction was finally defeated.

Chapter 4

HOPE Is Launched

Gov-elect Vandiver has vowed: "There will be no mixing in the classrooms come hell or high water ... the state won't be stampeded into choosing between no schools and integrated schools ... the plans he will offer the Legislature will not include any local option privileges."[1]
— Atlanta Journal-Constitution

Muriel Lokey was anxious to move the shoebox of cash and checks from under her bed to a bank account, but not in her name. The women knew they must find a name for the fledgling organization without the word "crisis" in it. They needed to convey optimism. Helen Bullard, a well-known member of Atlanta's progressive community, was invited to offer her unique voice at their next gathering. As the group's members threw out ideas for what to call the organization, and none of them seemed right, Bullard suggested HOPE — Help Our Public Education. The name obviously had a positive ring to it, and it was easy to say and to write. Thus, it was decided — they would call themselves HOPE.

Bullard, a spinster in her fifties, seemed an unlikely person to be the political guru that she had become in Atlanta. She had run Mayor Hartsfield's campaigns for ten years as a member of an Atlanta public relations firm, and her political advice was sought by both the experienced and neophytes seeking office. She was a familiar sight on city streets, smoking a cigarette while talking to someone, or as she hopped into a taxi. She had never learned to drive, and so she rode all over downtown in taxis, often switching cabs, so she could ask drivers their opinions on topics of the day. Listening to the pulse of the public added to her uncanny ability to read people — a necessary asset in winning campaigns. She had friends who were in the white power structure and she knew leaders in the black community. It was this bridge between the two races that had helped win Hartsfield black votes in tight elections. She was said to be the only Atlantan — man or woman — who could tell Hartsfield to be quiet and get away with it. Above all, Helen Bullard loved Atlanta. She once said, "If anything good spills over into the South, it comes from Atlanta."[2]

Muriel Lokey visited her local bank to deposit the checks and cash sent or given to her on behalf of HOPE. The bank teller asked Lokey for the names of HOPE's officers, a bank requirement for opening an account for any organization, but so far, HOPE had no officers. Lokey realized how little their group knew about the mechanics of starting an association.

A discussion soon followed among HOPE organizers. Maxine Friedman felt it was obvious that she could not be an officer. She was a Jew from New York City and her husband, an Atlanta businessman, did not share her enthusiasm for the cause. Muriel Lokey made it clear she could not have her name listed as an officer either. The group's goal was to keep HOPE removed from politics as much as possible and her husband was too well known in political circles. Fran Breeden seemed the logical choice. She had perfect credentials for the job: she was southern, having been born and raised on Florida's Gulf coast; Protestant; charming; articulate; and unknown in Atlanta. Breeden agreed to be Chairman of the Board of Directors provided Harry Boyte would take over as Chairman of the Executive Committee. He accepted the position with the understanding that the women would do most of the work. His professional life limited the time he could give to the cause.

However, the fact that Harry Boyte was a southerner from North Carolina and had years of experience in service organizations in Atlanta meant he could offer an authentic perspective to the impending school crisis. His contacts as Executive Director of the Red Cross (including leaders in business, finance, and medicine, and at churches and colleges and universities) resulted in some of these professionals serving on HOPE's Executive Committee and Board of Directors. These people lent respectability to the open-school movement, a smart and important priority for the founders.

Harry Boyte continued to seek and promote the active support from all citizens, in effect declaring HOPE a biracial organization. Although his position flew in the face of HOPE's assertion of neutrality in arguments over integration, in actual fact, HOPE's leaders were not genuinely neutral, because they were well aware that desegregation to some degree would come about if public schools were to remain open. They merely recognized that saving the schools would require rallying a public with deep, emotional commitment to segregation, and thus they could not appear to be promoting integration. Consequently, they separated segregation from the open-school movement, but it was a fine line to maintain. This tactical reasoning extended to promoting HOPE for whites, for only white citizens could reverse state policies. Breeden, who held unusually progressive views on race as a southerner, nevertheless became convinced during meetings in the Lokeys' living room that HOPE's mission had to be directed toward gaining support from white Georgians. But it was understood that unsolicited black support would be gratefully accepted. Frances Pauley finally decided to throw her hat in the ring, breaking her promise that she would never again join a whites-only group. She was convinced that since this was a political battle, and only whites held the power to decide the school question, she would join in HOPE's efforts.

Seventeen people gathered in the Lokeys' living room the night of December 8th, 1958 to draw up the charter for HOPE. James Dorsey, a former U.S. district attorney and a close friend of the Lokeys, explained the incorporation papers to the group. One of the few businessmen in the group made a recommendation that all of them sign a loyalty oath first. The gentleman said if they refused to sign the oath, he would resign and go to the press and tell them why he had resigned.

Hamilton Lokey explained that there was no reason for a loyalty oath. The group was simply exercising their rights in a free government for and by the people. The Constitution guarantees this right, he told the man, and the others agreed with Lokey.

Loyalty oaths had been in the public eye since the McCarthy hearings in which Senator McCarthy had sought to expose communists in the government. The oath included one's pledge not to engage in activities to overthrow the United States government. Jim Dorsey added that the McCarthy hearings, to his mind, had left a dangerous imprint in the public's mind. He thought the group should not honor that legacy by signing oaths. By the end of the discussion the businessman retracted his threats and signed the charter, and no loyalty oaths were signed. Jim Dorsey remained HOPE's legal advisor.

On December 15, 1958, an article appeared in *The Atlanta Constitution* entitled: "Hope Inc. Chartered to Fight School Close." The chartering group gave the following as its purpose: "To give factual information to those citizens of Georgia who want to keep our public education from being destroyed by the closing of our schools; to give direction, information and a program of action to those groups and individuals throughout the state who feel, as we do, that the closing of our schools would be a tragedy almost too terrible to contemplate."[3] The incorporators named in the charter were listed, three of whom were Mrs. Hamilton Lokey, Mrs. Harold Friedman, and Mrs. Thomas Breeden.

A manifesto signed by 311 white Atlanta area ministers on December 13, 1958 — almost four times as many clergymen as had endorsed a similar statement a year earlier — stated that it was time to "face up to the fact [that] enforced segregation in the public schools is now without support in and contrary to national law."[4] When surveyed by reporters, the clergymen said they would not allow church buildings to be used as classrooms if the motive was to circumvent court-ordered integration.

Governor-elect Ernest Vandiver gave a strong rebuke to this declaration by the clergy without mentioning the manifesto itself. He said Georgians "do not propose to be stampeded into a position where we will be forced to choose between mixed schools and no schools."[5] The ministers stated their opposition to mass integration or amalgamation of the races, but said that "some integration" would be possible in some schools "without insurmountable difficulty," though it would be inadvisable in others.

On December 21, 1958, 419 Atlanta-area medical doctors signed a petition to keep schools open, urging "whatever legal steps are necessary to prevent the closing of our public schools." The petition stated a school shutdown "would materially interfere with the supply of essential scientific personnel and this would ultimately damage the health services of this region."[6]

Professors from Agnes Scott College and Emory University joined local ministers and physicians in making public statements supporting the continuation of public schools. In November, 1958, Muggsy Smith, Fulton County representative in the Georgia assembly, began urging repeal of all Georgia segregation laws that called for setting up private schools. Representative Smith told an Atlanta reporter that the segregation battle had already been lost.

"It's now simply a question of whether or not we want public schools,"[7] he said. Smith added he was as much for segregation as anyone but he wanted schools to stay open for all children and would fight to keep them open. He also told the reporter that he had it on reliable authority that Atlanta would lose one-third of its teachers in the summer if they were not assured that schools would remain open.

Earlier, Smith had said a plan for the sale of Atlanta's public school buildings made more sense than any other plan advanced so far. The plan would be to sell the schools to private corporations, with state income tax deductions to assist parents to send children to private schools. The plan claimed it would probably cost parents $500 a year for each child attending a private school.

However, after carefully studying the private school plan, Representative Smith said he could not support it.

"It is impractical and unworkable. The only answer I see is repealing the segregation laws and leave it to individual counties to decide by referendum."[8] Smith was also aware that a private school solution to the crisis flew in the face of recent Supreme Court decisions in which any evasive scheme to avert the principles of the 1954 decision would be ruled unconstitutional.

Moving away from a private school solution, which Smith was convinced had "no legs," the Fulton County representative introduced a local option bill, permitting each school district to vote on "public schools or no public schools."[9] Maxine Friedman praised Muggsy Smith for again showing courage in the face of committing political suicide. His Spring Street school speech had already made him a pariah in the legislature except for the other members numbered among the "Sinister Seven" (the name given to legislators opposed to the resistance laws).

Just as the news hit the press about Muggsy Smith's upcoming local option bill, Georgia's Senator Richard Russell, in a speech before the Georgia Farm Bureau, slapped what he called the Georgia "surrender group" and promised that he would "never become a spokesman for those apostles as long as I have the strength to oppose them,"[10] and he made fun of those who proposed a "little integration."

During HOPE's early days, the group members had contacted open-school advocates in Virginia and Arkansas. The Virginia situation was particularly instructive. Under the Virginia resistance law, Governor Almond shut down schools in Front Royal, Charlottesville, and Norfolk at the beginning of the fall term in 1958 just as HOPE was organizing. These schools were still closed three months later, with about 13,000 children then receiving makeshift education in private facilities.

HOPE became the voice early on for all groups in Georgia who wanted to preserve public education — the League of Women Voters, Atlanta's Human Relations Council, and the Southern Regional Council. These organizations, in working toward improving race relations in the South, had been labeled by politicians and arch segregationists as too progressive, even "communist." They were

—AP Photo.

Mrs. Thomas Breeden (left), Mrs. Lokey . . . Paste HOPE sticker on car bumper.

"We Want Public Schools." January 11, 1959. Fran Breeden and Muriel Lokey. The photograph of HOPE founders spread across the nation soon after the organization debuted on the national stage. Courtesy of AP/Wide World Photos.

44

considered threats to the Georgia way of life. Therefore, in this fight, the only strategy that had any promise of success was the newly formed organization, HOPE, informing citizens of what was at stake, and publishing the resistance laws and court decisions and the likely consequences of both. HOPE made their position clear in a press release: "HOPE, Inc. does not propose to argue the pros and cons of segregation vs. desegregation, or states rights vs. federal rights. It has one aim — to champion children's right to an education within the state of Georgia."

On January 9, 1959, Judge Frank A. Hooper of the U.S. District Court in Atlanta declared segregated seating on Atlanta's buses and trolleys illegal. At about the same time, Judge Boyd Sloan of the same U.S. District Court ruled that the three blacks submitting applications to Georgia State College in Atlanta could not be barred from admission on the basis of race nor could qualifications be set up that were designed for that end.[11]

Governor-elect Vandiver called these decisions regrettable. He repeated his pledge to introduce legislation to the General Assembly in January "to prohibit mixed schools in Georgia anywhere, at any time, at any place."[12]

Frances Pauley, having made the capitol hallways and galleries her second home as a representative of the League of Women Voters, became HOPE's link with the legislature. She knew every bill before the house, the sponsors of the bill, and who voted for and who voted against the bill. Legislators, especially from rural counties, often disagreed with the League's positions and regarded the body as a radical organization, referring to the women pejoratively as "Leg of Women Voters."[13] The men Frances could corner were offered the facts and expert opinions on the issues before them. Sometimes she tried to persuade them to vote yea or nay on a particular bill, and spoke of what the consequences would be if the bill passed or not. Much of this engagement went on as the legislators walked down the halls from their offices to the floor or as they stood in groups smoking and talking between sessions — and sometimes inside their offices when she could maneuver entry. She did all this politicking without a care to fashion, except for wearing white gloves, a must for southern ladies at the time. The more gentlemanly legislators listened politely to her, knowing she was as well informed as any of their colleagues, and there were a few progressives who respected the rightness of the League's positions and regarded Pauley as an asset, especially during the school crisis. They needed all the support and help they could get to ward off the disaster they saw coming.

At the swearing-in ceremony for Governor Vandiver, Pauley took her usual seat in the gallery and stared down on the new governor, whom she referred to as "Little Ernie." After being sworn in, Governor Vandiver made good on his promise when he gave his "State of the State" address to the General Assembly on January 15, 1959:

"My first words to you are that your chief executive has no intention of turning Georgia schools and colleges over to the federal government for any purpose, anywhere, at any time during the next four years."[14]

The governor then proposed new legislation:

1. A bill to authorize the governor, as conservator of the peace of the state, to close a single public school within a system should it be ordered integrated, and to close the school from which the pupil was ordered to integrate. This was in addition to the power already possessed by the governor to close an entire affected system.

2. A bill to prohibit any political subdivision of the system having an independent school system from levying ad valorem taxation for the support of mixed schools. It was this bill in combination with the previous bill that would enable the governor to close Atlanta schools if a federal court should order them integrated.

3. A bill that would make the officials of any city or county school district operating mixed schools, regardless of the source of their funds, guilty of a felony to be punished under the law.

4. A bill allowing any city or county school board or governing body to lease school property for private educational purposes.

5. A bill making teachers in a privately operated nonsectarian school that affords education to children entitled to grants under state law eligible for pensions under the Georgia Teachers Retirement Act.[15]

The ceremony at the state capital for the incoming governor was covered in detail by the press. The extremist views expressed by Governor Vandiver motivated citizens of a more moderate persuasion to contact HOPE.

"First We Closed Our Schools, Then...." *Atlanta Constitution*, 1959. Clifford H. "Baldy" Baldowski Editorial Cartoons. Courtesy of the Richard B. Russell Library for Political Research and Studies, University of Georgia Libraries.

Many individuals called to offer their moral support to the open-school movement, and others donated their time and money to help the cause. The popular columnist of the *Atlanta Constitution*, Celestine Sibley, reported from the General Assembly as the body was winding down its 1959 session. One orator had just implored the assembly to keep the right to shoot firecrackers because it is "our way of life." A man standing next to her said, "We may have abolished the public schools up here this session, but let's by all means preserve the fireworks!"[16]

From the beginning of the fight to preserve school segregation in Georgia, there had been a band of representatives in the General Assembly who moved against the grain. They acquired the title "The Sinister Seven" because "time after time when one of the 'defiance bills' would come up for a vote, all the lights would be green (indicating a yes vote), except for the seven red votes of the Sinister Seven. These state legislators — Hamilton Lokey, James Mackay, Bill Gunther, Bill Williams, Fred Bentley, Bernard Nightingale, and Muggsy Smith — could not believe the length to which their colleagues were willing to go to safeguard segregation."[17] They began the fight against the rural bloc of politicians when the resistance laws were first introduced. Hamilton Lokey and James Mackay drew up a declaration stating that Georgia must have public schools. Only eight members of the General Assembly signed the document — the Sinister Seven and Hugh McWhorter. James Mackay coined the motto of the Sinister Seven: "I will not vote to destroy a living institution to preserve a dying one."[18]

Near the end of the 1959 General Assembly session, the floor leader, Frank Twitty, said, "It's the same story every time we try to pass a bill designed to preserve segregation, they [Smith, Reed and others] are opposed. We want to have segregation everywhere. We want it in Atlanta, in Dekalb County, in Cobb County and everywhere. ... The people of Georgia expect us to do everything we can to preserve segregation."[19]

Chapter 5

Women at Work

Georgia leaders have failed us miserably in handling the school situation.[1]
— Sylvan Meyer

In contrast to groups formed for open schools in other southern states, HOPE had been conceived as a statewide organization. Two counties (Fulton and Dekalb) were represented at the organizational meeting in which a provision was made in the charter for other chapters to have representation on HOPE's board of directors. It was decided in the beginning that HOPE would not be a dues-paying member organization, but instead, that supporters who might or might not contribute financially would be solicited for their time and effort. In a HOPE newsletter, the finance committee offered a monthly plan whereby supporters were billed annually, semi-annually, or monthly for their $5.00 per month contribution. This plan brought in more funds than a similar appeal that ran in a newspaper ad.

The group needed more money to run HOPE's comprehensive campaign than the dollars that drifted in, however. Maxine Friedman led the effort to approach Atlanta businessmen for donations. Her husband, a vice-president of an Atlanta manufacturing firm, gave her access to the business community, but she was turned down over and over with the same excuse — it was too early to predict the outcome. Clearly the businessmen did not want to stick their necks out on an issue so embroiled in politics. They had to gauge the political wind first to see which side was safest to be on, and to use another metaphor, Georgia politics and business had shared the same bed for generations. On her first attempt, Friedman collected from three donors — $200 was the highest contribution.

Friedman finally cornered Ben Massell, an acquaintance in her social milieu and real estate tycoon worth over $50 million dollars. He agreed to donate office space in the First National Building on Whitehall Street in downtown Atlanta. Another HOPE volunteer who knew Ivan Allen, Jr., then the owner of the South's largest office-supply house, asked this businessman to donate typewriters and other office supplies. Allen agreed, but he insisted: "Don't say a word about it to anyone."[2] Checks and dollar bills trickled in, with donors requesting that their gifts remain anonymous.

It was suggested at a HOPE executive meeting to put a little scare into the banking business by letting them know they had a stake in this fight. Stickers were printed to go on personal checks that read: "If schools shut down, this account may also close."[3] These stickers were widely distributed to HOPE supporters.

Nan Pendergrast, a mother of six, used her storytelling skills as the head of HOPE's speakers bureau. Although she often faced a stony silence in front of civic organizations, especially those whose members were predominantly male, Pendergrast maintained the easygoing confidence of someone raised in the well-connected, affluent Atlanta establishment. She made good use of her Atlanta pedigree in opening remarks when she said that her grandmother had the foresight to be born in the basement of the family home while Yankees occupied the rest of her house during the Battle of Atlanta. That story seemed to relax the men and engage their interest in the speech that followed. Pendergrast told her HOPE friends: "They were less likely to beat up a small Southern female." If she saw the audience was a bit more friendly than the status quo, she ended her talk with the story about a seven-year-old white boy whose family recently moved to Chicago from Georgia. The boy talked about his two new friends, Tommy and Billy, but, due to a new baby at home, the mother could not visit the school until Christmas. There she discovered that her son's two friends were the only black boys in the class. She asked her son why he chose them as friends, and he replied, "But Mama, all the rest of these kids are Yankees."[4]

The HOPE office quickly filled up with volunteer women lining up speakers, churning out press releases, and getting out their first mailings — reprints of legal interpretations of state and federal laws, educational and economic studies, speeches, fund appeals and informational flyers — to those on their mailing list, which grew every day. A list of HOPE projects was created and sent to individuals who expressed a strong interest in volunteering in their towns to spread the word of HOPE:

Telephone: Build a telephone tree. Ask ten people to get ten more people to get ten people who want to maintain public schools. Add these names to your mailing list.

Meet: 1. Hold small meetings, morning coffees, coke parties, luncheons to discuss HOPE. Informal groups in the back yard while mothers oversee small children's play. This can also be a "Dollar for HOPE" meeting.
    2. Have a big meeting or rally. This carefully planned with much publicity, newspaper, TV, radio, telephoning. This gets the information to a larger group since your publicity reaches many more than the meeting.

Petitions: Set yourself a goal and work for signatures on the petitions. 100,000 signatures from all over Georgia can influence the General Assembly session in January. As people are asked to sign, more people think and talk about public schools.

Observers: Have regular observers at your school board meetings. Try to learn more of the problems and help the board to consider planning ahead.

Mailing: 1. Publish a bulletin or newsletter. Mail to many people in your area. The state wide committee should help furnish news.
    2. Have a project in nearby rural areas where county mail boxes can be surfeited with HOPE literature. Many will read when they will not attend a meeting.

Literature: Put HOPE materials everywhere: Doctor's offices, Church meetings, Civic Club meetings. Educate!

Speakers: Form a speakers bureau. Don't wait for invitations, ask to be heard. Prepare well and the heckler will only add to the interest.

Organize: Organize a HOPE committee of at least five people in your neighboring counties. The voices of one or two in a community added to the multitude throughout the state will make a difference.

USE YOUR IMAGINATION! You know the best projects for your town.[5]

The key workers — Fran Breeden, Muriel Lokey, Maxine Friedman, Nan Pendergrast, and a few other women wedded to the cause from the beginning — would often start their day on the phone or writing press releases and answering written inquiries about HOPE before they headed to a meeting or to the office. All the women in the group added their HOPE responsibilities to an already busy schedule as wives and mothers. Before, during and after dinner, the phones could still ring, and the callers were not always friendly. Fran Breeden began to call some of the unfriendly callers, the "heavy breathers," because they would breathe heavily into the phone without saying a word and then hang up. Some callers, however, used expletives and called them "nigger lovers." In time, the ugly response to the group's attempts to save the schools would get worse.

A young man came up to Fran Breeden after one of the first public gatherings of HOPE, introduced himself as Bill Jones and offered to do whatever he could for the cause of open schools. Jones said he had just transferred to Atlanta with IT&T. Breeden took his name and number, later called him to help with fund-raising and thereafter Jones appeared at HOPE's office, at meetings, forums and other HOPE functions. The organization's need for people to help was so great at the beginning that no one bothered to look into backgrounds of those individuals who came upon the scene and offered to help. After many months elapsed, HOPE leaders noticed that Jones was not on the scene. He seemed to just disappear. Fran Breeden and others labeled Jones "the mystery man." He showed up many years later and related to friends the unverifiable story of why he had been a HOPE volunteer. He had been sent by the FBI to act as a mole within HOPE to see if the group had any affiliation with subversive causes.[6]

It was not long before the women realized the demands would soon be too much for volunteers. To spread the facts of this impending crisis across Georgia would require a mammoth organization and the skill of an experienced staff, but money was scarce. How could they afford to pay someone? Maxine Friedman and the men on the HOPE board of directors kept asking for donations from businessmen, neighbors, social contacts — those they believed were in favor of keeping schools open. But with the money coming in being spent on immediate expenses — like paper, postage, telephone bills and utilities — there was none left over to hire a staff.

The Southern Regional Council (SRC) came to their rescue. The SRC was not a well-known organization to most Georgians, but to progressive southerners, the Council had become a beacon of hope in improving race relations. In the early 1940s when the (SRC) was formed, the Council had tried to attack a wide array of social, economic and political problems in the South, but by 1951 its mission had narrowed to solving the region's racial problems. In that same year, the SRC openly stated its opposition to segregation.

Due to its public stand against segregation, it was necessary for the SRC to support HOPE behind the scenes, which prompted Harold Fleming, the director of SRC at its headquarters in Atlanta, to make an unusual financial arrangement with HOPE. Fleming had been contacted by a donor who wished to give monies to HOPE but to remain anonymous. It was decided that checks from the donor would be sent to a person not associated with HOPE and then forwarded to the organization. Fran Breeden's father, a lawyer in Florida who had handled private trusts for many years, became the conduit.[7] Fran Breeden learned several years later that a young mother who was married to a member of the famous Mellon family had made the anonymous donations. Her eventual fate as a passenger in a plane that disappeared over the Caribbean Sea has remained a mystery.[8]

HOPE's biggest challenge was to dispel the complacency entrenched across the state and to do it in a sufficiently dramatic enough way that the attention of the average citizen was captured. A public rally was planned for March 4, 1959, in the Tower Theater on Peachtree Street. Volunteers worked at a frantic pace sending invitations and publishing the first newsletter in February. "FILL THE TOWER WITH HOPE," a promotional flyer, went to the press, to PTAs, to chapters of the League of Women Voters, women's clubs, law and business groups, and any person or group who expressed an interest in saving the schools.

The massive publicity paid off. Nearly every seat in the Tower was taken. Approximately 1,800 people attended, and there was statewide print, radio, and television coverage. The speakers sitting on the stage with Fran

Breeden were Atlanta's Mayor William B. Hartsfield; *Atlanta Constitution* editor Ralph McGill; Sylvan Meyer, a young newspaper editor from the *Gainesville Daily Times;* Mrs. Gordon M. Wilson, of the Little Rock Emergency Committee; and a student from a local high school who had organized an open-school group among high school students. A few blacks were seated in a section set aside for them near the front of the auditorium.

Fran Breeden, standing at the podium in front of all these faces, felt a rush of anxiety, just as she remembered always feeling before going on stage as an actress. She had wanted Harry Boyte to run the meeting, but he had boosted her confidence by insisting that she was a natural mistress of ceremonies. He knew she was the best person to be seen representing HOPE by the people of Georgia.

She began her opening statement extending a welcome to all at the first public meeting of HOPE, which was being held to discuss the school situation in the state. She recognized the delegations that were sitting in the audience from Marietta, Smyrna, Austell, Gainesville, and other Georgia towns. She then explained that the purpose of HOPE was to inform citizens of the challenges facing the electorate and of the real dangers of closed schools in Georgia if its citizens remained complacent and ill informed. Breeden made it clear that the potential school crisis was not confined to the city of Atlanta, but rather, would affect the entire state. The impending school crisis was Georgia's problem and HOPE's belief was that ordinary citizens like the ones seated in the audience held the key to keeping public education strong and viable in the state.[9]

Breeden and other HOPE leaders expected to find hecklers in the auditorium, but none were heard. At the end of her speech, Breeden received an enthusiastic round of applause. It had been arranged for city police to stand guard in case of a disturbance, and no one in HOPE knew it at the time but IT&T (International Telephone and Telegraph) workers who had signed up as HOPE volunteers had arranged for 200 plainclothes guards to be in and around the building. Only two people had to be removed from the premises.[10]

Popular Mayor Hartsfield was introduced to loud applause. Not known for being a mealy mouth, Hartsfield told the audience that the "outhouse crowd" (his description of hate-mongers) had better stay out of

Atlanta or they'd "get their heads knocked together." The mayor said that closing the schools would be a disaster — that businesses would fold and quit coming to Georgia's fair city if managers and employees could not educate their children.

When Breeden introduced Ralph McGill, the audience clapped so long that McGill had to ask the audience for quiet so he could introduce the young editor from Gainesville, Sylvan Meyer. Meyer represented the voice of the New South, of those young and ready for change. With his good looks and butch haircut, he could have been mistaken for a University of Georgia football player.

"Georgia leaders have failed us miserably in handling the school situation," Meyer told the audience. "They have set their course to chaos and they are committed. They began by telling us they needed laws to close schools.... And they told us schools would never close because of these laws. In their intense sincerity, they were wrong. The doctrine of state sovereignty died at Appomattox and was reentered at Little Rock."[11]

Meyer, feeling the crowd was with him, said that the attitude about closing schools was changing, "imperceptibly, but changing. A new leadership is emerging in Georgia. Slowly, slowly, new arguments are reaching the public ear. For me the dilemma is over. If I have to choose between public schools and no public schools, between enlightenment and ignorance, there is no dilemma.... This will be called 'surrender,' but I assure you fighting for the life of Georgia's public schools is not surrender. It is the new offensive."[12]

Meyer's use of the term "surrender" referred to the repeated cries from diehard segregationists in newspaper articles, letters to the editor and on radio and TV that went like this: "Georgians don't surrender to outsiders. They can't tell us how to run our state. Keep up the fight."

Meyer declared that none of Georgia's laws setting race as a criterion for school placement would hold up in a court of law.

"The governor knows this.... I can only interpret their legalisms as a form of mild hysteria that blocks the normal logic of their minds."[13]

In closing, Meyer said: "HOPE may persist and win. It may fade away. But it has started something that is bound to persevere, come what may."[14] He returned to his seat to thunderous applause.

Remarks from Mrs. Gordon Wilson of Little Rock — a young woman with short black hair, big expressive eyes, and a serious demeanor — injected harsh reality to the assembly.

"We were lulled into believing there would be no trouble in Little Rock. We took it for granted that our schools would remain open,"she said.[15] She made it clear that the children had been hurt badly by the four high schools closing. She described makeshift classes in old buildings with mostly unqualified teachers.

"High school students are restless and discouraged. It wasn't only the children that were affected by our schools closing. The whole city's been affected. The most thriving business in town is the long-distance moving companies."[16]

Wilson cited a survey conducted by the Little Rock chapter of the American Association of University Women, which disclosed that 44 of 85 businessmen interviewed felt that the school closing hurt business in Little Rock.[17] Breeden wondered how anyone, after hearing Bobbi Wilson describe the dire situation in Little Rock, could sit back and not become active in HOPE.

Kim Hodgson, a junior at Druid Hills High School, was introduced. Hodgson told the audience that "the majority of the students in the Atlanta area want public schools."[18] Hodgson said that from the student viewpoint, the "closing of schools would be one of the greatest disasters to befall this community."[19]

Harry Boyte closed the rally with a short speech. His remarks centered on the objectives of HOPE. "First, HOPE wants to awaken the citizens of all 159 counties in Georgia to the imminent danger to all schools in our state.... We want to make Georgians everywhere realize that this is not just a crisis here in Atlanta, where a suit is pending and where the decision is expected."[20]

He described HOPE as an organization through which voices could be heard in the crusade to save schools. In his third objective, Boyte announced an action program HOPE planned to pursue, if a "public school anywhere in the state is closed because it has been ordered to desegregate, HOPE will lend support and encouragement to action designed to reopen that closed school."[21]

There were some HOPE volunteers in the audience who shuddered at Boyte's third objective. The Executive Committee had discussed the possibility of lending support in the event of a closed school in a cursory fashion, but at HOPE's debut many thought it was best to leave out any potentially controversial point that could be played up and misconstrued by segregationists and amplified by the media.

Boyte ended his address with upbeat optimism, however. "We believe that HOPE offers a realistic and truly American way out of this crisis. We hope you will join in this historic battle, the most significant in the South of the 20th century."[22] He said that if Georgians showed common sense and wisdom they could set an example for other southern states and the free world.

"That is why we ask you to stand up and be counted. That is why we ask you tonight to help spread HOPE through Georgia!"[23]

The audience clapped and clapped. The buzz was on. The entire evening's program was broadcast live on local radio and summarized on the ten o'clock TV news. Many people lingered in the hall, talking with friends, or with strangers sitting next to them. Some people went up to the stage to ask questions of the speakers. Some stuffed HOPE flyers in their purses or in suit and coat pockets. Many left the Tower Theater that night, alarmed and ready to offer their time and/or their money to the cause. Fran Breeden, Muriel Lokey, Maxine Friedman and other HOPE leaders felt a surge of optimism generated by the Tower audience. They had started a movement.

Helen Bullard phoned Muriel Lokey the next morning to say: "The dome at the Capitol is rockin'."[24]

In fact, HOPE meant more trouble for the dyed-in-the-wool segregationists than they could possibly have imagined at that time, but the Tower rally aroused alarm and gave HOPE respectability with open-minded moderates. The event organizers had started a wave of public interest and every day more and more Atlanta citizens wanted to ride the wave. This high-profile meeting also meant the members of HOPE were the targets of hate mail and hate telephone calls by the "lunatic fringe," but there were also public denouncements from respectable Georgians, like Governor Vandiver and Senator Richard Russell.

Chapter 6

Tea and Bigotry

If the white people of the Atlanta area stand united, Negroes will get nowhere with their integration efforts.[1]
— Roy Harris

The rallying cry heard from the podium of the Tower Rally worked. Phones rang at the HOPE office. People were full of questions — What could I do to help? How could I organize a chapter in my town? Where should I send money? The same kind of inquiries rang Fran Breeden's phone as well as other officers whose names had been announced on the air and in the newspapers.

An excited inquiry came from Beverly Downing of Athens, Georgia. She was fired up from the rally and wanted to know how to organize a chapter. Although Athens was the seat of the University of Georgia, it was still first and foremost a southern town with old-time southern values. But Downing believed she could start with a few open-minded individuals associated with the university. Soon she had brought together a small group of prominent Athens residents who were in favor of keeping schools open. In an effort to publicize the open-school movement to a wider audience, the group sent invitations to the principal organizations in Athens to a meeting at the local country club to hear two leaders from Little Rock speak about the problems they faced with school closings. This organizing group, which became the Athens chapter of HOPE, wondered if anyone would come. "You just didn't do this sort of thing in Georgia or you might get a cross burned in your yard," Downing recalled years later.[2]

But to HOPE's surprise, the event drew a huge crowd to standing room only. Downing realized they had hit on a winning strategy to bring out the people. If citizens knew that well-respected members of the community were involved, they would feel safer and more inclined to participate. Margaret Shannon, a reporter from the *Atlanta Journal*, came away with a compelling story of old, established Athens awakening to the school crisis.

Athens and other chapters forming across the state needed support from the office that was already swamped with work. HOPE's executive committee had discussed the urgent need for additional staff and with the financial support coming from a Southern Regional Council source, the officers agreed to pursue the hiring of an executive director for the organization.

Harry Boyte was asked to search for a suitable candidate to fill the position of executive director. With Boyte's connections in the city, he was the one most likely to find a qualified person with sufficient organizational skills to oversee the entire operation of HOPE. Boyte believed they needed a real professional with experience in leadership roles, preferably in not-for-profit agencies. The candidate should be able to deal with all sorts of people, who had initiative and be a problem solver. But who would sign on to this challenge with an embarrassingly low salary?

Boyte reported a week later that he had the right person for the job, but the candidate, Betty Harris, had requested a conference with Breeden and other officers before signing on. After such a meeting Harris was hired. Boyte had known Betty Harris through Atlanta's Human Relations Council and from events at Quaker House. She was one of the few white citizens in the Atlanta area who had been working for racial equality for many years. As a Girl Scout professional, she tried with little success to plan interracial programs and day camps. In the early 1950s, she arranged for her friend, Lillian Smith, the outspoken, anti-segregationist Georgia author, to speak at a convention of Girl Scout professionals at the Georgian Terrace Hotel in Atlanta. The event did not please many, including Ralph McGill who refused the invitation to speak along with the controversial author.

Betty Harris spoke with a genuine southern voice as a Georgia native.

She had the advantage over many recent newcomers to Atlanta in facing this deep-seated emotional issue with her fellow Georgians. She came from a family of Methodist preachers and educators and through her professional life developed contacts across the state, which later became an asset on the job.

With Fran Breeden's input, the new executive director kept her eye on the ball, tackling the most urgent head first — to keep HOPE's momentum going that began with the Tower Rally. They must generate news. They must remain in the public eye.

Harris, along with Frances Pauley, her former Agnes Scott classmate, began to organize teas to be held around the city, hosted by women in their homes. The hosts invited neighbors, friends, and especially women with school-age children. The tea strategy was twofold. HOPE was spreading up-to-date information about the reality of school closings in Georgia to small groups where people of divergent opinions might feel comfortable enough to discuss the issues in this familiar southern setting of afternoon tea. The other advantage of teas as Harris and Pauley saw them included arranging media coverage of the teas, which would be spreading HOPE's mission farther afield.

In late April the *Atlanta Journal* society section ran a photo of Pauley and two other well-dressed women, wearing white gloves, pouring and receiving tea from a silver tea service. The caption underneath the picture read: "Parties galore — At the first of a series of sixty parties to be held within the next few days by HOPE ... to spread information about public schools throughout Atlanta and Georgia."[3] The added benefit of the teas meant coverage fell in the society pages of the newspapers. Many women skipped hard news but never failed to look at the society section.

The tea idea caught on. It became a catalyst for others wanting to volunteer for HOPE to bring their neighbors, old school friends and PTA acquaintances together to inform them about the real threat of schools closing. Some of the volunteers only agreed to hold these gatherings if their names were not released to the media. They feared harassment from hardline segregationists, including "crazy fringe elements."

Open-school advocates were not encouraged to read Ralph McGill's article in the May *Saturday Review* in which he wrote: "There does not seem to be much hope of avoiding closing the schools ... most of the politicians care more about their own political face than the children."[4] Many in HOPE felt McGill had his finger on the pulse of the public and knew the Southern mind as much as anyone.

A group of six Atlantans had just obtained a charter for an organization devoted to keeping public schools in Georgia segregated, calling themselves Metropolitan Association for Segregated Education, Inc. (MASE). The organization claimed over five thousand members by 1960. In its charter, the organization proposed to "provide a forum for the dissemination of truth relating to the education system of this state."[5] The other opposition group to desegregation of schools, Georgians Unwilling to Surrender (GUTS), was led by Lester Maddox, who also started the White Citizens Council in Atlanta. HOPE sent Maddox an invitation to join their organization, asking him for a donation to keep the open-schools movement going. Maddox was not amused. He returned the flyer with a confederate bill, writing on it that this was more than they deserved. Both opposition groups made sure the HOPE office was kept up to date with their newsletters and flyers.

The more informed Atlanta segregationists had reason to worry about the outcome of the NAACP suit against Atlanta's board of education. If Judge Hooper could rule that segregation of Atlanta buses was unconstitutional (January 1959), then what might he decide in the school issue?

Georgia Congressman Erwin Mitchell of Dalton, Georgia, sent out a press release and made a television appearance in Atlanta with an urgent message to Georgians: "The adult citizens of Georgia should make practical plans now to open private schools next fall in case the Georgia public school system fails."[6] Mitchell reminded the people of Georgia that they had made their decision through the ballot box not to have integration in the public schools.

Marietta, Georgia took Congressman Mitchell's advice and obtained a private school charter for white students to open in the fall of 1959. Other affluent communities across the state were starting to plan for private schools.

There were days when Fran Breeden read columns and letters to the editor and wondered if HOPE had a chance against the ignorance and naiveté of the public. The politicians had been feeding the people for so long on thick pabulum of half-truths and outright lies that she feared the so-called "school crisis" was being treated as irrelevant background noise.

Tea parties organized in towns across the state generated publicity about HOPE, which was good news. But along with the publicity came crank calls to anyone named as associated with the open-school movement. Muriel Lokey received a call from a Columbus, Georgia, woman who said she had heard that people trying to keep the schools open in Atlanta were Communists. She didn't want any part in a Communist plot. Before Lokey could speak, the woman hung up the phone.[7]

A well-publicized keep-the-schools-segregated rally was held in Atlanta a few weeks after HOPE's Tower event and during the tea parties. Roy Harris, former speaker of the Georgia Assembly from Augusta, Georgia, president of the white supremacist Georgia States' Rights Council, and no relation to Betty Harris, bellowed to the crowd of some 700 people that Negroes want to call off efforts to integrate Atlanta schools but "renegade" whites are blocking their efforts. Harris incited the audience to harass "Raustus" McGill (editor of the *Atlanta Constitution*) and Ham Lokey. He reminded them McGill was the number one enemy of states' rights and integration supporter. Harris and Lokey were longtime political foes, dating back to Lokey's term in the state legislature.

"White people must stand united to make sure Negroes get nowhere with their integration efforts. There'll be no race-mixing."[8] Harris pounded his fists on the podium as he shouted. The crowd roared with furious clapping, yelling, "That's right. A-men."

During the mass meeting, the telephone numbers of Ralph McGill and Ham Lokey were given to the audience: Harris told the crowd to give them a call and keep them awake all night.

The phone rang at 3 o'clock A.M. the next day in the Lokey house. Hamilton Lokey picked up the phone beside his bed and heard a heavy "breather" on the other end. He read about the segregationists' big meeting, so he knew the "breather's" source. Remembering that Roy Harris stayed in the Henry Grady Hotel when he was in town, Lokey dialed the hotel. The switchboard operator asked:

MUST WE INTEGRATE TO EDUCATE?

NO!

HEAR

THE LAW and FACTS

EXPLAINED BY

HON. CHARLES J. BLOCH

Nationally recognized Constitutional Attorney and others—

MONDAY, MARCH 2ND

8:00 P.M.

SANDY SPRINGS HIGH SCHOOL

Presented by

NORTHSIDE ASSOCIATION TO CONTINUE SEGREGATED EDUCATION

Poster by Northside Association to continue segregated education. Courtesy of HOPE/Lokey Papers, Atlanta History Center Archives.

"Are you sure you want to disturb Mr. Harris at this hour?"

"Oh, yes. He's expecting my call."

Harris answered the phone in a sleepy voice.

"Who is this?"

"Ham Lokey," he said amiably.

"Well, hey, Ham."

"I'm sure you want to know your boys are working. I'll report to you each time I get a call, just so you know."[9]

After that exchange, the Lokeys received no more calls from "the boys."

There was a positive flip side to the virulent opposition to HOPE. Every time Roy Harris or Lester Maddox made a speech or ran an ad in the newspaper for segregated schools or no schools, cash and checks flowed into the HOPE office.

Georgia's teachers delivered a more sobering blow when they voted two to one at their convention in late March to support the continuation of separate but equal schools. The vote came after a bitter fight on the convention floor between a small number of moderates, largely from Atlanta, and representatives from rural counties. HOPE knew it was a bad omen to have teachers willing to close schools across the state rather than desegregate them, however gradual the process might be. Governor Vandiver spoke at the convention promising he would try his utmost to assure pay raises for them despite a shortfall in the state education budget.[10] The governor whose election was based on never allowing the races to attend the same schools and the teachers' self-interest brought them together as codefendants of the status quo.

A few months later, *The Augusta Courier* published a Roy Harris editorial addressed to the school teachers and school officials of Georgia:

"There has sprung up in Atlanta a spurious organization known as HOPE, Inc. HOPE is trying a squeeze-play. They are trying to mislead the people of Georgia into believing they have one choice and one choice only. They say that we must accept race mixing in the public schools or have no school at all. ... Now their position is a fraud on its face."[11]

Harris went on to say that the NAACP isn't satisfied with what the courts are doing in the South. "They will not be satisfied with anything less than complete and massive race mixing."[12]

Brit Pendergrast, the husband of Nan Pendergrast, was stopped by the state patrol while traveling from Columbus, Georgia, back home to Atlanta. On the back fender of the Pendergrast station wagon read the sign, "We Want Public Schools." It was early evening before dark, but the officer cited Pendergrast for nonfunctioning headlights and gave him a ticket.

Throughout the episode, the patrolman talked in strong words against all those people in Atlanta forcing our children to sit with "negras" in schools.[13] His fiery condemnation came straight from the Roy Harris playbook. The open-schools stand taken by the Pendergrasts affected their family on a more personal level when their daughter was not asked to make her debut in Atlanta, as Nan and her mother had done in the past. A warning was circulated that went like this: "Don't ask that Pendergrast child, she'll bring a black to the Piedmont Driving Club."

In June of 1959, HOPE held an open session of its executive committee, which turned into a turbulent debate. A former candidate for governor, Arthur Neeson, started the lively argument by asking Chairman Fran Breeden: "Hasn't HOPE weakened our stand?"[14] Neeson had run his campaign on "perpetual segregation" and asked that "we fight as a race of people against the Negroes and money-makers" who are trying to integrate the schools. Someone in the audience answered a reference Neeson made to "those who fought in the war" with the statement that he fought for the United States of America, not Georgia. The crowd applauded. Breeden ended the meeting by saying the discussion (Neeson's argument) was not within HOPE's province. "We want our schools open; we're not concerned with anything else."[15]

Reverend Robert B. McNeill, a Presbyterian pastor in Columbus, Georgia, was dismissed in June 1959 after a bitter racial dispute of several years duration. The minister had made public statements in regard to helping blacks attain "first class citizenship" and asked that white citizens work out racial problems with Negroes, not for the Negro. Upon learning that he was fired, McNeill explained that the dispute started after the church had organized a Negro congregation in the city. The controversy grew worse upon discovering they could not find a black preacher for the new congregation. McNeill hired a retired white minister to preach at the Negro church.[16]

HOPE garnered mixed results from the clergy. Some individual ministers supported the open-school movement, but in the beginning of the struggle there were not many who made their views public with the exception of the manifesto signed by Atlanta ministers in 1959. Betty Harris called on Methodist Bishop Arthur Moore to ask for his support. After

Harris gave her introductory talk in which she included that her grandfather had been a Methodist preacher in north Georgia, the bishop responded, "Mrs. Harris, remember, I have to be bishop to all the people. I cannot be in the forefront of this because I am bishop to all Methodists in Georgia."[17]

Harris left Bishop Moore, again discouraged by the lack of moral leadership from Christian leaders. In an earlier conversation with her own minister of the First Congregational Church in Atlanta in which Harris had asked him to make a public statement in support of open schools or to address the problem from the pulpit, he responded in a similar manner as Bishop Moore. "There is too much feeling on both sides. I have to minister to all our church members."[18]

HOPE leaders formed a motorcade of twenty women from several open-schools advocacy groups to call on Senator Talmadge at his Lovejoy, Georgia, farm. Upon their arrival, Mrs. Talmadge served coffee to the ladies and then the senator asked if anyone wanted to speak, adding that "Mrs. Breeden said she would be alone. I didn't expect all these people." Fran Breeden fumed inside, knowing she had said no such thing.[19]

DELEGATES OF OPEN-SCHOOLS GROUP MEET WITH SEN. RUSSELL
Shown With Senior Senator in Winder Are Mrs. Paul Keller Jr., Mrs. Edward Vinson

"Open-Schools Advocates Meet with Senator Russell." February 8, 1960. Senator Richard Russell (left), Mrs. Paul Keller, Jr. (center), Mrs. Edward Vinson. Courtesy of Bill Wilson/ *Atlanta-Journal Constitution.*

Many in the group asked the senator sticky questions and the answers revealed the politician that he was. Betty Vinson, representing the League of Women Voters, asked him if he still supported a private school plan in Georgia. The senator hemmed and hawed, never answering the question. Fran Breeden left Lovejoy with an overwhelming sense of disgust at the Georgia senator's devotion to segregation.[20]

Another convoy of open-school advocates visited Senator Russell at his home in Winder, Georgia, enduring the same frustrations they encountered in Lovejoy. The senator did not enjoy the pounding he received from open-school advocates and insisted, as he faced Betty Vinson, "That blood will flow in the streets"[21] before desegregation takes place. Vinson answered she was sure he would use his power and prestige to help see that no blood would flow and that peaceful change would occur. Margaret Shannon, who was present at the Winder meeting, wrote a column in the *Atlanta Journal* about these visits, which showed that Georgia senators had been singled out and pressured by open-school advocates.

Frances Pauley was furious when HOPE colleagues found one of Herman Talmadge's "dirty tricksters" taping a HOPE meeting at the Ansley Hotel in Atlanta. Pauley found him hidden in a little room where the speaker system was located. HOPE personnel had announced before the meeting began that taping the event was not allowed. Pauley knew the trickster as the photographer who took pictures of black and white people and spliced them together to promote the segregationist agenda of fear and anger over race mixing. Pauley spoke to the man and convinced him to turn over the tape rather than be arrested.[22]

HOPE officers and others in the movement knew they were up against politicians like Roy Harris and other like-minded segregationists. But when the Ku Klux Klan was mentioned at a HOPE Board meeting, Maxine Friedman, a no-nonsense New Yorker and a practical voice in HOPE, said they shouldn't waste any energy or time worrying about these ignorant malcontents.

Soon afterward, Maxine Friedman had to eat her words. She picked up the phone one day to hear a malcontent threaten to burn a cross on her lawn. She waited with her camera ready. A car arrived in front of her house. Two men got out of the car quickly, stuck the cross on the lawn and zoomed off.[23]

The Friedmans disconnected their phones for a while after the cross incident. From the beginning of HOPE, Maxine Friedman did not tell many people she was Jewish.[24] Being Jewish in the deep South carried its own risks and she did not want to hurt the cause she believed in so passionately.

The Klan was especially known in rural counties and had a history of "in-your-face" intimidation and worse. The Klan, revived in the 1920s, had designated Atlanta its Imperial City. But the city moved away from that single Klan designation by the 1930s when it became the home of a Commission on Interracial Cooperation and a radical grassroots organization, the Association of Southern Women for Prevention of Lynching. Lynching had disappeared in Georgia by this time, but not Klan activity as HOPE volunteers were learning.

Chapter 7

Courts and Politicians

The state of Georgia simply cannot secede from civilization.[1]
— Hamilton Lokey

The "good old boys" in Georgia politics might have regarded Frank A. Hooper, a southern Georgia boy, as one of them — a segregationist to the core. He grew up in Americus, a farming town tied to the roots of Georgia's racial history. By the mid–20th century, white and black relations had not changed much since the Reconstruction era. Whites employed blacks in their homes as maids, cooks, and yardmen. A few blacks farmed their own land, but most were still tied to the white "boss" as a tenant farmer. Some older black men stepped aside for whites to pass on the town's sidewalks. Most whites knew nothing about how or where black children went to school.

Hooper represented Americus in Georgia's general assembly in the 1920s. He began his career on the bench in 1943 as a state superior court judge, remaining in that position until 1949 when he was named to the United States District Court in Atlanta. In 1959 Hooper was 62. Whatever the judge's personal views on the school issue happened to be, they would not sway him from upholding the law of the land.

The NAACP suit, *Calhoun et al. v. A.C. Latimer et al.* filed in the clerk's office at the United States Court of Appeals for the Northern District of Georgia on January 11, 1958, included 10 plaintiffs against nine Atlanta Board of Education members and Miss Ira Jarrell, the district superintendent. The plaintiffs, led by Vivian Calhoun, sought an end to segregation in the Atlanta public schools, not individual admissions to white schools.[2] NAACP lawyers entered the Atlanta fray armed with plaintiff wins in federal court decisions that grew out of the Little Rock controversy. The Atlanta petition stated:

> the rights here sought to be protected are rights secured by the equal protection clause of the Fourteenth Amendment of the Constitution of the United States and Title 42, United States code, Section 1981. This is a proceeding for a preliminary and permanent injunction enjoining defendants from operating the public school system of the City of Atlanta on a racially segregated basis.[3]

The plaintiffs' legal team of well-respected local black attorneys, E. E. Moore, Jr., Donald Hollowell, and A. T. Walden, joined the NAACP in pursuing the case. Constance Baker Motley had assumed a prominent role in taking the Atlanta case this far. Motley, a protégé of Thurgood Marshall, had become a seasoned litigator in civil rights by 1958. She had come down to Jackson, Mississippi, from New York in 1948, her first experience in the Deep South, to argue a case with her NAACP colleague, involving pay equalization for black teachers. One day during the trial, Motley and her colleague stopped at a grocery to buy fruit for their lunch. The owner stood talking to a white customer, ignoring the black customers. Finally he asked, "Something I can do for you, boy?" Motley realized that if she said anything contrary to the white owner, she could die on the spot and nothing would be done about it. The two left with the understanding that any black who became the least bit assertive could face the threat of violence. The Deep South mores never left Motley's consciousness.[4]

The Board of Education hired some of the most able lawyers in the city to defend their position of separate but equal schools. "Buck" (B. D.) Murphy headed the team with Newell Edenfield and J. C. Savage assisting.

Two of the Negro parents who were part of the original suit to end segregation in Atlanta public schools withdrew from the case in May 1959. The remaining parents made a joint statement at the time that they "intended to go on with the suit and wanted the schools desegregated for the benefit of their children."[5]

On Friday morning, June 5, 1959, one and a half years after the plaintiffs' petition was filed in federal court, Judge Hooper read a preliminary order before the court (prior to legal argument). The judge ruled in favor of the plaintiffs. He ordered the Atlanta school board to cease operation of segregated public schools and to present "within a reasonable time" a plan for integration.[6] Judge Hooper did not have the power to order integration of the schools, but he did have the power to end segregation.

During the day-long hearing, Judge Hooper indicated he viewed the process of change as token integration or as a gradual move to desegregating the schools. Miss Ira Jarrell, Atlanta's school superintendent, testified that the city had "tested children of both races and found the achievement level of Negroes trailed those of whites." She added that the school system was experimenting with ways to bring black children up in their achievement scores. It was apparent from Judge Hooper's follow-up questions that he viewed Jarrell's testimony as an admission that the Atlanta schools were already taking steps toward token integration.[7]

In a sense, blacks in Atlanta had been working toward real equality since they came from working the red clay fields of Georgia to finding a better life in the city of opportunity. Their struggle is littered with small victories and big disappointments. Improvement in education had always been prominent with black crusaders. Now, with the *Brown* decision in place, and with the help of NAACP legal personnel, some degree of better schooling was within grasp. A look back tells the story of a resilient people who kept "their eyes on the prize."

* * *

The separate-but-equal schools policy in Georgia had followed the separate part, but never the equal. Black children studied from old and often dirty textbooks with ragged or missing pages. School science labs were under-equipped, and many classrooms needed repair to walls, ceilings, and desks. In this segregated society in which whites saw blacks as domestics, yardmen, or passengers in the back of the bus, what kind of schools black children attended did not enter the minds of ordinary white citizens, just as most white Atlantans knew little about the "other Atlanta" that included the most highly rated black university system in the country.

Public education in Georgia had a checkered past with standards that ranked near the bottom of the country for many decades. If white children received inferior schooling, then one can only imagine the conditions of black schools. The historic problem in establishing primary and secondary education in the state was rooted in the state's ambivalence toward allocating meager state funds to educating its children, as well as the unwillingness to school nearly one-half of Georgia's children during the time of slavery, when state law prohibited the education of blacks. Although the Georgia constitution of 1777 had a more liberal view of education, requiring schools be supported by the state (whites only), that clause was dropped by later state constitutions. Fortunately, political leaders had the foresight to charter a state university in 1785 (University of Georgia in Athens). At the same time, the state tried to adopt a system of free schools, but there was not enough revenue to support them.

By 1869, during the third Reconstruction of Georgia, Republicans in both Georgia houses enacted "a thorough system of common schools with the requirement that county school authorities shall as far as practicable provide the same facilities for both races."[8] Atlanta and a few of the more densely populated towns had established their own locally supported systems by 1880, which contained the better public schools in the state. Eventually, the local systems were given a share of the school fund. By 1900 there were approximately fifty local systems.[9] Rural schools barely got by with allotments from the Poor School Fund. Affluent families sent children to private academies, most of which were of high quality and expensive. The "equal facilities for blacks" segment of the common school law was generally ignored by the white political structure until eighty years later.

A short-term Progressive era at the turn of the nineteenth century produced the school fund as the largest item in the state budget, and a compulsory attendance law enacted by the Georgia legislature in 1916, which was largely unenforced.[10] The bulk of Georgia's children lived outside local systems with their schools financed by the common school fund. In the plantation counties, most of the funds went to white schools, enabling the local establishment to provide education without local taxation. The black schools were the most financially deprived in the state, but at that time the general view was that blacks and sharecroppers did not need an education. In 1905 the 12 public high schools in the state were for whites only, with the large majority of graduates going on to college.[11] In 1910 Georgia spent $1.76 per black child for black teachers' salaries and $9.58 per white child for white teachers. Not until 1926 did the Georgia legislature create a small school equalization fund to aid the poorest counties and districts. In 1936 Georgia had 431 white public high schools and 40 for blacks.[12]

The Yankee boot on Georgia soil left a bad taste in the mouth of those who lived through it, and they passed it on to the generations that followed. The populace rejected the idea that outside forces, i.e., government, had any business meddling in local affairs, including support of schools. Educating children was the responsibility of local communities or churches. This residue of resentment of Yankee's fed into the already pronounced "southern rugged individualism" of those who lived off the land. Georgia's rural dominance in state affairs accounts for the ups and downs of support for public schools during its history until the middle of the twentieth century.

In Atlanta before the Civil War, the educational budget situation for blacks was minimal as it was in the rest of the state. In 1853 the state's Poor School Fund financed several academies, one high school and a music school for Atlanta's white children. It took the Civil War to bring about opportunities for blacks. The Freedman's Bureau, a Reconstruction program, opened two free grammar schools for black children in Atlanta in 1866. The American Missionary Association (AMA) sent white teachers from the north to run these schools — Stoors and Summerhill. At this time these were the only free schools available for either white or black children.[13]

Soon thereafter the black Baptist church opened an academy, with other churches following. Classes were held in church basements. It was a haphazard system that left large numbers of black children uneducated.

The president of the Atlanta City Council, Dr. Daniel O'Keefe, an innovative leader and a post–Civil War resident of the city, agreed with the governor and proposed a resolution calling for the establishment of a free public school system within Atlanta city limits. All the political in-fighting among council members revolved around members who believed it was proper for the city government to support schools versus those who felt the responsibility for educating children should rest with parents. In 1869 an agreement was reached to submit a bond issue. It passed with little opposition. The Atlanta public school system opened in 1872, with three grammar schools for whites only, two for black children, and two high schools for whites only. Summerhill and Stoors were public in name only; for they were still supported by the AMA.[14]

Amy Williams, a teacher at Stoors since its beginning, asked the city board of education what was to become of her graduates? They responded that students "should pay their tuition at the normal (Morris Brown) if they wish to attend high school."[15]

The city council misread the public, thinking that most citizens would not want the government building and running more schools and that most girls would not be interested in attending school. Parents whose children were left out demanded that schools be built, forcing a second bond issue. This time it was defeated by black voters.

The fight to defeat the bond issue was led by a black city councilman, William M. Finch, for these reasons: All the money from the first bond issue was spent on the white schools. The two grammar schools for black children remained in railroad boxcars in which classes were held with one teacher to fifty students. Most black families could not afford the fees to send their children to high school at Morris Brown Normal School.

The city council president pleaded with Reverend William Finch to convince the black voters to pass the next bond issue by promising he would do all he could to appropriate funds for the two existing black grammar schools, to have a black high school built, or make arrangements for student tuition to be paid to Morris Brown and to build additional grammar schools

On good faith, black voters helped to pass the bond issue. Delays in fulfilling the city council promises prompted Cyrus Francis, a member of the First Congregational Church, and Edmund A. Ware, Atlanta University President, to threaten a legal injunction against the school board if they did not see action soon on getting black schools under the public domain. In late January 1872, board members voted to assume support of the black schools (Stoors and Summerhill). But they would not agree to building additions to the schools, only to pay teachers' salaries.[16] The strategy of the black leaders was clear. It was better to get half a loaf than none at all.

They had to wait fifty-two years before a black high school was built in Atlanta. Booker T. Washington High School opened in 1924.

By 1874, black leaders in the community began petitioning the school board to hire black teachers for their grammar schools. These petitions were ignored by the board, whose intentions were to eventually hire all southern white teachers because they "will instill into (black) minds proper Southern ideas and teach them the proper relation that exists between them and the white race."[17] Once blacks had learned that proper relation, the board could "educate teachers of their own race" and turn schools over to them.

There was one point on which the white city fathers and the black community leaders agreed. Both wanted to get rid of the AMA teachers from the north. The AMA had established the First Congregational Church in the black community. Ministers from traditional black churches felt their membership threatened by this "outsider group." White city leaders objected to the northern teachers as being "religious scoundrels who are poisoning the minds of the colored people and raising them so much above their proper position that they will not be house servants any longer."[18]

A spokesman for the AMA responded to the city officials: "The colored people so dislike the southern women that there will not be that mutual respect between teachers and parents that is essential to the welfare of the school."[19]

Ultimately, money decided the issue. School bonds did not always pass and there were scant funds in the city coffers to pay teachers and keep up the buildings. It was still a common view that parents should be responsible for their children's education. The Board realized they could save money if they began to hire one or two black teachers each year and see how they worked out. They would pay black teachers less than their white counterparts.

In the fall of 1877, two black teachers taught in the public schools.

Black teachers were required to be natives of the South and residents of the state.

Official school documents read : "The races shall be kept separate in the normal school (Morris Brown) as well as in the schools." The same year AMA was removed from Atlanta's public schools, "ridding themselves of every taint of Yankeeism."[20]

In 1881, Atlanta ended integrated public school faculties. The black community had been pushing for this autonomy, furthering the proposition that whites and blacks must be segregated.

The *Atlanta Constitution* wrote in 1887 that hiring all black teachers for black schools would encourage greater segregation. "The fight of the Negroes of this city for colored teachers confirms ... the inevitable drift of things between the races." Other Georgia cities found hiring black teachers for black schools "works to admirable advantage."[21]

Black students were turned away every year between 1873 to 1887 when there were three black grammar schools in the city. "To pay school taxes and never be able to get a child in school" was a constant complaint. The ratio of students to teachers remained high: 50 to 1, 51 to 1, 59 to 1.

In 1896 whites had 17 school buildings; blacks had 5. At that time blacks made up 43 percent of the population. In a little over thirty years blacks had gone from a slave status in which education was forbidden to the acknowledgment by Atlanta's local officials that blacks were entitled to an elementary education at public expense. It was considered progress by the black community.

By the time Atlanta began desegregating its high schools, racial equality in the city had improved under the leadership of John Wesley Dobbs and Austin T. Walden. The two men had organized the Atlanta Voters League after the 1944 Supreme Court ruling that the all-white Democrat primary was unconstitutional. The black leaders had gone to Mayor Hartsfield before he turned more moderate in race relations and asked for black police officers. The mayor responded without hesitation that they would get blacks on the force about as soon as they'd get black deacons in the First Baptist Church (white). Dobbs and Walden cornered Hartsfield again with the request. Hartsfield responded, "When you get me ten thousand votes, I'll listen to you." In 1948 with votes in hand, they negotiated with the mayor and were rewarded with eight black policemen. Black leaders kept up the pressure on the city leadership and in 1958 golf courses were desegregated.[22]

In 1953 the Voters League used its political capital and elected the first black member of the Atlanta school board, Rufus E. Clement, President of Atlanta University. In 1958 the gap between dollars spent on white and black students had narrowed since the early 1950s after more money had poured into black schools to shore up the argument that the state provided equal opportunity to both races. Still, fewer dollars were spent on black students — $226.35 per white student; $187.78 per black student.[23]

* * *

The day after Judge Hooper's preliminary ruling in favor of the plaintiffs, the headline in the *Atlanta Constitution* morning edition, June 6, 1959, read: "Court Orders Atlanta Plan for Integration of Schools."

One could almost hear the "rattling of sabers" among politicians and the general public as the news spread over the city. Senator Richard Russell joined in the public outcry, stating: "I hope that the Atlanta school board will use every means at their command to resist this effort of the itinerant lawyers of the colored peoples association."

Reporters talked with the people — in barbershops, in coffee shops, in hotel lobbies and on street cars to measure the public's reaction to Judge Hooper's ruling. No one wanted to be quoted, but an informal survey found that most Atlantans' feelings ran counter to Judge Hooper's ruling. Mayor Hartsfield was quoted in the paper the next day, pleading with Georgia's general assembly to grant Atlanta citizens the local option in working out the fate of their integration-threatened public schools. In private conversation, the mayor swore at state legislators for trying to destroy the city he loved so passionately.

HOPE hurriedly organized a public meeting in Atlanta to discuss the Hooper ruling, to defuse the sting of the word "integration" from the public mind to the issue of keeping schools open with local option being a realistic alternative to the massive resistance laws enacted by the Georgia legislature years before. Fran Breeden with her most active volunteers had been listening to Hamilton Lokey who said all along that Judge Hooper would uphold the law of the land. He did not have a choice. It was the politicians HOPE had to work on and there was no other way of influencing them than through the people who elected them. "The state of Georgia simply cannot secede from civilization," Lokey said.

Eleven days later on June 16, Judge Hooper, filing his final judgment after hearing the case argued before the court, ordered the Atlanta Board of Education to submit a plan by December 1 of that year for desegregating its schools.[24] Allowing this much time for the board to submit a plan, the judge opened a window of opportunity for politicians to avoid the collision course headed their way. Hooper stated that operating segregated schools in Atlanta violated the Fourteenth Amendment: "To make any other ruling would only add to the confusion which already exists in the minds of so many of our good citizens, and the build up in the breasts of our citizens hopes of escape which would soon be torn to shreds by rulings of our appellate courts on review."[25]

Opening the mail every morning at the HOPE office could be a mixed blessing. Often there were checks enclosed ($100 from Eleanor Roosevelt), letters supporting HOPE or those volunteering to serve in some capacity. Other envelopes contained strong opposition to HOPE.

Soon after Judge Hooper's ruling appeared in the papers, HOPE ran a full-page ad in *The Atlanta Journal* with a statement of HOPE's purpose and a call for Georgia citizens to not let their representatives destroy public schools. One day the office received a copy of the HOPE ad inside an envelope with a message written across the page in red ink:

"All I hope is You and your kind will move to Africa. Why don't you openly join the NAACP with Mayor Hartsfield?" signed, "A true Georgian."

On July 18, 1959, *The Atlanta Journal* ran the headline: "Atlanta's School Board to Appeal U.S. Ruling Outlawing Segregation." The board president, A. C. Latimer, had until August 9 to appeal the case.

James Dorsey, a former state attorney who had advised HOPE on legal matters from its inception, and Hamilton Lokey assured HOPE leaders that the appeals court would not overturn Judge Hooper's ruling. The appeal was pro forma.

Iris Blitch of Homerville, Georgia, who represented the south Georgia district in the United States Congress, told reporters that Atlanta should get busy and organize private education.

Mayor Hartsfield told the media that Atlanta could do better than the disaster when Little Rock desegregated its Central High School, not by blocking the inevitable but by being smarter and enacting local option, so Atlanta could decide whether to close the schools. He told the legislature it would be a grave mistake to hold Atlanta "hostage" and warned that if the comprehensive resistance laws remained, state institutions — Georgia Tech and the University of Georgia — would close.[26]

Ralph McGill (editor of *The Atlanta Constitution*) came out in favor of local option. He had written in February of 1959 that the myth had been perpetrated on the citizens of Georgia that state legislatures, state courts and governors had the power to override the constitutional interpretation of the U.S. Supreme Court. McGill thought there had been a slight sobering of public opinion since the Supreme Court shot down Virginia's private school option.

The mayor, Ralph McGill and more progressive Fulton County representatives were still up against the same political machine that had been running the state for decades. Roy Harris and other like-minded politicians discounted news that ran counter to their cause. They believed Georgia was too proud of its history to fall into traps that had plagued Little Rock and Virginia. *Life* magazine ran stories in consecutive weeks on "The Lost Class of '59," concerning the fallout of school closings in Norfolk, Virginia. There were pictures of boys hanging out in a drugstore, of cheerleaders practicing on a sidewalk for a football season that did not happen, and student leaders praying for a resolution of the crisis. The Norfolk schools opened two months later due to a suit initiated by black parents.[27] Georgia politicians could not escape the harsh reality of going against federal court decisions. But there were many who were still in a state of denial.

HOPE used the Little Rock and Virginia examples to their advantage. Nan Pendergrast nabbed volunteers, many women who had never spoken in front of a group, to go before civic, social and alumni organizations to make the point that Little Rock and Norfolk could happen in Atlanta if Georgians refused to make their representatives face reality as federal court decisions became clearer by the day.

In November 1959, one month before the December deadline announced by Judge Hooper, the Atlanta Board of Education presented their desegregation plan to the court. It was an effort toward minimal change to the status quo, within the confines of the Hooper ruling. The plan called for a rigid pupil placement concept with eighteen criteria that had to be considered in any school transfer request, including student potential, availability of transportation, classroom space, and possible impact on the community in regard to violence, unrest or economic retaliation. In addition to the many transfer requirements, the plan stipulated that applications for transfer would only be made available May 1 with the deadline for their submission May 15. Only twelfth-graders could apply the first year, eleventh- and twelfth-graders the following year, continuing with an additional grade per year for the next twelve years.[28] It was the least the Board of Education could do and still fulfill the Court's mandate.

Judge Hooper approved the Board of Education plan, but postponed its implementation until the General Assembly convened in January 1960. He wanted to give the legislature an opportunity to change its mandatory school closing laws.

Chapter 8

A Solution or Delay?

This distinguished group of men ... reflects the shadow of paternalism that ... loomed over Georgia.[1]
— Jeff Roche

Governor Vandiver found himself with two options, each holding an element of appeal and potential disaster. He could disobey the court, deny Atlanta its school funds and in essence close its school system. This action would make him a wildly popular hero with rural and small-town populations of the state. But this option did not have a long-range positive effect, because of the threat of federal charges against the governor, and also, the parents of the closed Atlanta schools would surely force the issue back to court as HOPE had promised in numerous press interviews and in direct communication with the governor's office. In court again, Judge Hooper would have no choice but to order the governor to reinstate school funds or to close every school in the state. This outcome would severely damage the state's educational system and ruin the governor politically. His other option was to make a case for the preservation of education and allow Atlanta to desegregate its schools. This action would bring Vandiver national prominence and make him a hero in Atlanta but a traitor in the rest of Georgia. This option also threatened him with criminal charges from the state because as the present laws stated, the governor must suspend funding to any "mixed" school. The governor was between a rock and a hard place.

The governor also had political ambitions beyond Georgia as an ally of John F. Kennedy in his race to the White House in 1960. It was necessary for him to hold onto the control of Georgia's Democrat party in order to deliver the state's electoral votes to Kennedy. Roy Harris held an inordinate amount of power for someone out of elected office who could challenge Vandiver if given the right issue. On the one hand, Vandiver had the "Harris bulldogs" yelping for segregation at any cost, representing the bulk of Georgia's Democrat party and on the other side, he had the courts, Mayor Hartsfield, and HOPE snapping at his heels to keep public schools open. He needed Georgia Democrats to win the state for Kennedy and his chance for a position in his administration. But the tide had turned in the country against the South, which could doom Vandiver's national ambitions if Georgia's resistance laws against a federal court order remained.

Another factor adding to Vandiver's predicament concerned the possible benefits of a private school system, saving the state enormous sums of money, and the added attractiveness of controlling the school curriculum and eliminating liberal ideas.

By the end of 1959, Governor Vandiver stood nearly alone among Georgia's foremost political leaders. Senator Herman Talmadge withdrew his vocal support of private schools, citing its unworkability. The senior Senator Richard Russell, who had been on record denouncing any kind of desegregation throughout his career, suddenly became silent on private schools. They foresaw that the political winds were changing. Both senators also were convinced the state would lose support from the business community with an unworkable private school plan.

There was still no way a rural representative to the state legislature could tie himself to urban interests and survive politically. Therefore, all bills for local option introduced by Fulton and Dekalb representatives were voted down by the overwhelming majority in the assembly.

Governor Vandiver, who held a law degree from the University of Georgia, could not imagine himself not upholding the law and defying a court order. As he put it, "Well, you either had a choice of seceding from the Union and we had tried that before, not being successful, or you had to obey the laws of the Supreme Court. [You] either followed the law or you didn't follow the law."[2]

HOPE had managed to break the silence on the school crisis by the time the 1960 legislative session convened. Letters were sent by local open-school supporters to their legislators covering nearly all 159 counties, which must have appeared as though HOPE was a mass movement across the state. But in reality, these letters may have represented one or two people. In spite of progress made so far, HOPE was not optimistic about the eventual outcome. There had been an avalanche of letters to the editors of Georgia newspapers declaring "war" on HOPE, articles by pro-segregationists and ads from Separate Schools including an invitation to send in one dollar "to keep WHITE schools WHITE."

Frances Pauley and Betty Vinson, the women who knew the state legislature from years of experience with the League of Women Voters, realized it was touch and go in the historic battle before them. They were fighting raw emotion embedded in the psyche of the southern white whose belief in segregation was as rock solid as the granite of Stone Mountain. The southerners in HOPE encountered these powerful feelings in their own families and friends, who in many cases denounced HOPE's views or refused to speak to them on the issue.

HOPE had produced 20,000 names on a petition for open schools at the end of 1959. The number reflected success in organizing chapters in many sections of the state. Fran Breeden, Betty Harris, Frances Pauley and other HOPE "insiders" were pushing toward a groundswell of support for open schools by the opening of the legislature in January 1960. Beverly Downing, chairperson of the Athens HOPE chapter, sent an open-schools petition with 740 signatures to Governor Vandiver.[3]

Downing called a press conference on the steps of the state capital on opening day of the General Assembly. She stood at the top of the marble steps, unfurled a scroll of signatures of open-school advocates, a list long enough to land on the pavement below.[4] Television cameras and print reporters crowded the scene. Just as HOPE had planned, the image of the scroll of open-school supporters at the state capital flashed across the evening news and was reported in the next editions of local and out-of-town newspapers.

Governor Vandiver continued with his campaign promise in publicly maintaining his stand that no desegregation would take place during his administration. But behind the scenes Vandiver admitted the pressure was increasing daily. He had asked his closest advisors: How could he get out of this "hornets' nest" without losing face? The governor's team of lawyers, including Buck Murphy, Charles Bloch, and Holcombe Perry, were instructed to travel the South to talk with their counterparts about various local option plans, pupil placement programs and other strategies to maintain as much segregation as possible. Vandiver became convinced that Georgia knew as much as other southern states. Therefore, the governor believed the people just had to learn the facts and vent their frustrations. He delegated the problem to his chief of staff, Griffin Bell, instructing him to come up with an idea to meet those criteria.

Days of the 1960 session passed. Still no legislator came forward to introduce a bill to change the massive resistance laws on the books. Behind the scenes, Griffin Bell followed up on the governor's desperate call to do something to postpone a collision with the court. He proposed that the legislature find out how the people of Georgia felt about desegregating — "go to the people and let them decide" — a tactic that might get the monkey off Vandiver's back.

When Frances Pauley and Betty Vinson (state president of the League of Women Voters at that time) heard the proposal of going to the people was being discussed at the governor's office, they thought "it's about time." They had made appointments with the governor, which were repeatedly canceled. Finally, Vandiver met with the women who made the suggestion to provide a means for the people to voice their opinions on the school issue. Now it looked as though the governor might go ahead with such a plan.[5]

Governor Vandiver believed going to the people would stir an intense public debate, resulting in the demand for a popular vote between "either integrated public schools or no schools."[6] Such a vote would relieve the governor of all responsibility on deciding the issue.

Neither the governor nor his staff could propose Griffin Bell's idea to the assembly. It had to come from a legislator. The leaders in the assembly and Governor Vandiver decided on George Busbee, a representative from Dougherty County in south Georgia. He lived in the county seat, Albany, a small city on the Flint River, where HOPE had experienced difficulty in organizing support for open schools.

84

The men who selected Busbee reasoned he would not be accused of pandering to any one interest. The assemblyman was not affiliated with the leadership of the House or Senate. He would present the bill independent of political pressure, so went the rationale for selecting him. Governor Vandiver, on a hunting trip near Albany weeks before the 1960 legislature opened, gave a copy of the bill to create a study commission to the local Democrat Party executive, James Gray, who was a rabid segregationist. He, in turn, gave it to Busbee and swore him to secrecy about the governor's involvement.[7]

After much arm-twisting, Busbee introduced the bill that became known as the General Assembly Committee on Schools. The bill proposed that the committee hold public meetings in all ten of Georgia's congressional districts, allowing witnesses to express their views on the school situation, and after the hearings, report its findings and recommendations to the General Assembly.[8] Georgia was the first state to propose state-wide public hearings.

Representative Busbee was reluctant to introduce what he knew would be a controversial bill. He was convinced his political career would be over after the people of Albany heard of his involvement.

HOPE needed a reliable state-wide organization in order to quickly notify open-school supporters of what was happening in the capital, with the governor, and the courts. From the beginning, HOPE had tried to reach out to all Georgians, but the results had been scattered. As events began to heat up in the school struggle, it became essential to make a coordinated effort and travel the state to form HOPE chapters in as many counties as possible. Frances Pauley, Beverly Downing and Betty Harris spearheaded the effort.

Betty Harris had worked as a Girl Scout professional in the north Georgia counties of Hall, White and Habersham, and in the Flint River area of south Georgia. She and Pauley made trips together, using their contacts where they had them and when not, they found a local phone book, called ministers in town and schools to ask for names and numbers of PTA officers. Often Harris or Pauley talked with someone who agreed with HOPE's efforts ending with, "but I'm the only one that feels this way." They found that "I'm the only one" response amounted often to several

"I'm the only ones," which gave Pauley and Harris the chance to organize a meeting of these reluctant women. They met in Sunday school rooms, living rooms and sometimes over coffee or lunch in a local eatery. Some of these women were afraid to discuss HOPE with their husbands or extended families. After one of these organizing trips, if only one person in a town had been found to support HOPE they counted their effort a success. That one individual would receive HOPE mailings with up-to-date news on the school crisis with encouragement to pass it on to friends and neighbors. HOPE slowly formed a communication channel through which the latest news pertinent to the cause eventually reached every corner of the state. The most important message HOPE conveyed was that this was not an Atlanta crisis, but a crisis for all school districts in the state. The hot button words *race, segregation* and *integration* were not used in HOPE brochures, press releases or in communication with volunteers. Just as Maxine Friedman announced during the organizing meetings of HOPE, the issue was about keeping Georgia's public schools open and not about preaching the merits of desegregation. Although there was dissent on the policy, it turned out to be a shrewd tactic.

Fran Breeden could not remember a time when she was this busy. She was either on the phone, attending a meeting or at the office constructing HOPE's plan to bombard the General Assembly with open-school supporters when it opened in January. Along with other HOPE women, Breeden barely had time to grocery shop or do the laundry. The hate calls kept coming. One call prompted Breeden to try reasoning with the caller but it was of no use. In tears, Breeden phoned Mary McGill, the wife of Ralph McGill of the *Atlanta Constitution,* asking for her advice. McGill wisely recommended that she never attempt to reason with these ignorant people. "It won't do any good and will do you harm." She added that the McGills had been enduring these abusive calls and threats for many years.[9] From then on, Fran instructed her children not to answer the phone. She hung up at the first abusive word.

Mrs. Dorothy Tilly, a Methodist pioneer in civil rights, represented church women in HOPE. She tried to hold no animosity toward these "misguided" folks who phoned her. As soon as she heard the ranting and raving on the other end, she played a recording of Bible verses. It did not take long before the caller hung up.[10] Another volunteer heard from a Ku Klux Klanner so many times who kept saying he was coming over to burn a cross on her lawn that she finally said to him, "Go ahead and come over. I'd like to see how big a cross you have." She fretted a bit afterward but the cross never came.

HOPE's legislative committee meticulously planned how to pack the gallery with open-school supporters on opening day and each day following for the duration of the 1960 legislative session. Members of this committee had been working to find volunteers from Atlanta and from other Georgia towns who were willing to be gallery spectators at the capital and to buttonhole their representatives any way they could catch them — in the hallways, on elevators, in the coffee shop, or to making appointments with their secretaries. It made sense that legislators would pay more attention to their own constituents than to HOPE's home office.[11]

Letters were sent to each committee member with precise instructions regarding which days they were to serve as HOPE representatives in the gallery to answer questions from spectators about the legislature or about HOPE. The committee members were advised that if they were approached by the press, they were to inform them they were individual members of HOPE, not authorized to speak for the organization, and to refer the media to any one of the three HOPE officers or the executive director. One of these individuals would be in attendance at the legislature at all times. The committee members were also advised in the letter: "HOPE's one and only position at the moment is to favor any legislation which will keep schools open. It is not backing any particular bills at the moment. Please keep a non-partisan attitude on other matters brought up in the Legislature."[12]

Frances Pauley, with the help of Judy Neiman and Betty Harris, made sure HOPE literature was placed on every legislator's desk several times a week during the session. The operative word was "saturate" the representatives with open-school propaganda.

HOPE spectators — all women — wore hats and white gloves and sat quietly in the gallery. They had recruited enough volunteers to almost fill the spaces available for the public. HOPE's main thrust came on the day of the legislature's traditional joint session when both United States Senators, Richard Russell and Herman Talmadge, made their annual appearance to address the Georgia lawmakers. On that day HOPE spectators arrived early to pack the gallery. As the senators were escorted into the legislative hall, everyone on the floor stood and clapped. Usually the senators heard applause and cheering from the upper gallery, but this day there was an uncomfortable silence. The two men looked up and saw the women wearing hats and sitting with their white gloved hands in their laps, staring down at them. Senator Russell stepped to the podium to address the crowd, Frances Pauley who stayed on the floor, gave the signal to the gallery. They stood, pulled out their hidden signs and held them up: "WE WANT PUBLIC SCHOOLS." Everyone on the floor looked up and glared at the quiet demonstration. It was against the rules of the house to carry placards or signs in the gallery. HOPE volunteers had made their signs and hid them inside their coats.[13]

After seeing that HOPE had packed the gallery, the opposition quickly marshaled their forces to show the Assembly their support for segregation. On the far edges of the gallery seating, a few raised signs reading, "WE WANT SCHOOLS TOO BUT SEGREGATED."[14]

Griffin Bell and Ernest Vandiver decided that the Committee on Schools should be composed of prominent citizens of the state. They tightened the selection process by hand-picking statewide organizations whose presidents would sit on the commission. Bell did not want to "leave it to chance who would be on the Commission." The groups designated to serve included the Farm Bureau, the Superior Court Judges Association, the Georgia Chamber of Commerce, the Press Association, and the Georgia Municipal Association. Well-known members of the educational community were also represented, including the heads of the board of regents and the educational cabinet, the chancellor of the university system, and the state superintendent of schools.[15]

Governor Vandiver searched with extreme care for the best man to head up the commission. His choice finally came down to John A. Sibley, former judge, counsel for Coca Cola, and president of Atlanta's Trust Company Bank. Griffin Bell, who worked for the law firm of King and Spaulding where Sibley was a partner, asked Sibley on behalf of the governor to lead the commission. There were aspects of the proposal that caused Sibley concern. He was afraid the Committee on Schools would be viewed as only a way to delay desegregation and would not receive the proper support from the governor or the assembly. Bell gave his assurance that the committee's only purpose was to find a solution to the school crisis. Sibley then agreed to chair the committee. After Sibley told Bell he was president of the University of Georgia Alumni Association, that group was added to the list of organizations represented on the committee.[16]

As soon as word was out that John Sibley would head the Committee on Schools, Mayor Hartsfield expressed the feeling of others who knew Atlanta's power structure. Bill Hartsfield had maintained a close relationship with the biggest business in town — Coca Cola — throughout his years as mayor, which meant he knew John Sibley well when Sibley served as Coca Cola's councel. He believed Sibley was the right man to chair the committee on schools.

John Sibley was not only very active with the University of Georgia alumni, but he had been a prime player in Atlanta's business community. Supporters believed Sibley would use all his energy and expertise to save the state from disaster.

The distinguished members, all white men, selected to sit on the committee reflected the paternalistic tenor of the times in the deep South. It was believed that the state's citizens would view the school crisis as a serious matter if these highly respected men were willing to serve on the commission. The blue-ribbon panel should impress Judge Hooper with the sincerity of the assembly's efforts.

The vigorous seventy-one-year-old John Sibley was the perfect embodiment of the old southern patriarch and the New South businessman. As Sibley put it himself, "I felt I had been a lawyer and businessman and could see [their] point of view, a city man and could see theirs, and a country boy and could see theirs. With this background I could ask people for their views on the question without making them mad."[17]

Sibley, born in 1888, had a southern pedigree that few could rival as a descendent of the Confederate war hero, James Longstreet. He grew up on a farm in Milledgeville, Georgia, earned a law degree from the University of Georgia while running a small farm to pay his expenses. He practiced law in Milledgeville before being asked by Atlanta attorney,

Hughes Spauling, to join his law firm during World War I. Sibley fought the legal battles of Coca Cola, as the company's general counsel, during the 1920s and 1930s. He took over as president of the Trust Company Bank in 1946, resigning in 1959 to retire to his farm north of Atlanta. Perhaps his most important job lay ahead as the chairman of the commission on schools, which later became known as the Sibley Commission.

Although some praised the selection of John Sibley, there were others in HOPE who felt it a hammer blow — more of the same old-line Georgia politicians who backed Vandiver and his stand against desegregation at any cost. These doubters thought the commission's purpose was either to stall for time or to convince the people to maintain resistance. One politically astute observer maintained the commission was created for "show," allowing the citizens to express their opinions but the outcome had been predetermined by both Sibley and Vandiver.[18] Most people had forgotten or had never known that Sibley opposed the *Brown* ruling, once writing that "throwing the races together" would take away racial differences and encourage miscegenation, which would result in a "mongrel race of lower ideals, lower standards, and lower traditions." He felt the Supreme Court had overstepped its boundary and should be curbed from interfering with "states rights."[19]

The HOPE women who were wary of John Sibley were glad to learn that two men serving on the commission were members of the anti–Talmadge faction: John Greer who had fought the Ku Klux Klan in trying to pass an anti-mask bill in the General Assembly, and Judge Samuel Boykin, president of the Superior Court Judges Association. Both men had served the more moderate governor, E. D. Rivers.[20]

The morale of HOPE's leaders lifted with what they deemed their window of opportunity to spread the open-schools agenda through the political process. They recognized that John Sibley represented most whites at the time, which gave his chairmanship a level of acceptability to the electorate so crucial to the success of the committee's mission. HOPE took heart from Sibley's conviction that not even segregation should override ethical legal standards, public education, or a thriving economic climate.

The 1960 legislative session ended in February. The Sibley Commission hearings were set for March. HOPE switched gears from politics at the capital to finding the right people willing to testify for open schools at all ten hearings of the commission. There was so much work to do that the women who started HOPE did not take the time to appreciate what the organization had already accomplished. The phones kept ringing, and there were important meetings to organize, press releases to write, and mailings to go out. Everybody was tired. Yet morale remained high. Most everything in these volunteers' lives took a back seat to their commitment to HOPE. Many Atlanta leaders, not affiliated with HOPE, gave the group credit for making the Sibley hearings politically feasible.

The capitol building was crawling with reporters and cameras, an impossible situation for the commission to carry on their business. After their first planning meeting they moved to the boardroom of Atlanta's Trust Company Bank. The members decided that only Sibley would speak for the commission, giving all interviews and answering questions from the press. One member recalled: "The press was hounding the hell out of us."[21]

Sibley helped the members to design a plan for public hearings that would convince Georgians to support changes in state law that would allow the desegregation of Atlanta's schools. This task would only work if the panel could assure the rest of the state that they would not face a similar situation. To ensure this result, the commission submitted for public approval a new form of resistance, adopting every known legal method of preserving segregation. Their other important job was to fully penetrate the silence that still surrounded segregation and resistance. They could only accomplish this by adopting a HOPE strategy: define the issue sharply and eliminate any arguments for or against the practice of segregation.

The commission planned each of the ten hearings to begin with testimony from representatives of groups that had held meetings, taken polls of their members or conducted open forums on the school question. This procedure would ensure that widespread discussion on the issue would occur before strong opponents of desegregation could voice their emotional objections, which could set a negative tone from the start. Making sure that organizations participated in the hearings gave the commission an indication of how many more Georgians felt than it was possible to hear from individuals. Groups were urged to bring their results of discussions and polls to the hearings or mail them in beforehand.

To keep the state's focus on the commission's work, all ten hearings were scheduled during the month of March. It was in the commission's interest to shorten the events, to create a sense of urgency, generating intense interest.

John Sibley decided to offer two basic options to hearing witnesses: to continue resistance at the expense of public education in order to preserve absolute segregation, or to change state law to preserve public schools and the maximum amount of legal segregation. Sibley hoped by narrowing the discussion to these simple choices, Georgians would see the folly of continuing their massive resistance and discard a private school plan.[22] Also, this plan would allow the "hot-heads" to blow off steam in a controlled environment.

The 159 counties in Georgia were grouped under ten congressional districts. An effort was made to select a hearing site most central to each district. School gymnasiums and courthouses were used to accommodate the numbers of people the commission expected would attend the hearings.

Sylvan Meyer assured Fran Breeden, "You [HOPE] deserve credit for the school study commission ... since only your constant and brave presence at the legislature could have convinced our august solons that the rumors some want the schools open is true."[23]

Chapter 9

Let the Hearings Begin

It's mind changing time all over Georgia.[1]
— Sylvan Meyer

The commission held the first hearing in Americus, deep in the heart of the Black Belt region of the state. In the Black Belt, which cut a swath down the middle of the state, nearly every county had a black population of 45 percent or more. Chairman John Sibley and John Greer, who scheduled the hearings as secretary of the committee, made a calculated decision. They would go first where whites were most resistant to desegregation in order to gauge the extent of hostility toward the commission; thereby not providing more time for their harsh opinions to fester while hearings were being held in locales more sympathetic to change.[2]

The core volunteers of HOPE, who were busy preparing their supporters around the state to attend and testify for open schools, were split in their assessment of the motives and probable outcome of the hearings. Fran Breeden agreed with Muriel Lokey and Betty Harris that these hearings could be HOPE's validation for all the groundwork of their many dedicated volunteers. But Frances Pauley, the most astute political operative in HOPE, questioned why the commission decided on such a hurried hearing schedule. She suspected they had a motive, counterproductive to open-school advocates, but she held her fire until after the first hearing.

John Sibley drove down the icy highway from Atlanta to Americus during the early hours of March the third. The Third Congressional District included twenty counties that were largely farmland with one major city, Columbus. Citizens across the district were also making their way to Americus on this cold morning to speak their minds or to witness the event. Some came unshaven, wearing overalls and others were well dressed, many with their "speeches" to the commission clutched in their hands. Once inside the small courthouse, they were instructed to file a written request to testify with Secretary Greer.

Chairman Sibley called the meeting to order at 10 o'clock sharp. He announced to the gathering there would be no "speech making" at these hearings, that if the school question was put to a vote, that would be the time for debate and argument and emotions. Sibley, fearful of a violent reaction to the commission's questions, worked to create a calm atmosphere. He read his thirty-minute statement in his soft, middle–Georgia drawl. He carefully explained Georgia's school situation. He told the Americus audience that the Supreme Court had overstepped its bounds in the *Brown* decision. He called it "devoid of legal reasoning and sociological validity" but nevertheless demands Georgia's compliance. He gave the history of Judge Hooper's rulings, reminding the people that the loss of public education in the state was a grave possibility the way the laws were presently written. He told the crowd that separate schools could still operate and that integration was not an absolute.

The chairman's statement was meant to hit all the potential hot button issues, especially to calm the fears of whites that their children would be forced to attend mixed schools. Local option was the escape hatch. Let Atlanta choose minimal desegregation to comply with Judge Hooper's ruling while the rest of the state continues to operate unchanged.

Sibley spoke directly to the blacks in the audience, seated in a special section of the courthouse. His comments centered on what he deemed was their self-interest: With desegregation blacks could lose their right to educate their own children, and their school system of thousands of black teachers, principals, administrators and bus drivers would disappear. Then he spoke to the whites in the crowd not to hold "our local negroes responsible for the tensions and ill feelings that are being engendered between the races," stating they were "the innocent victims of false leaders, some misguided, some influenced by sinister motives, and many pursuing subversive purposes."[3]

Arguably the most important part to Sibley's statement came at the end when he presented the people with their options. The first was to do nothing. Atlanta would desegregate its schools, the governor would cut off funds to the school district, the parents of the affected children would probably file suit to reopen the schools, the federal government would force Governor Vandiver to reinstate school funding to Atlanta schools or close every school in the state whereupon the education system would be converted to a private organization. He made it clear to his listeners that the state could have nothing to do with the private system, state property could not be used, and grants-in-aid would be Georgia's only obligation. Private schools would have to be built, organized and staffed. He asked them to consider the possibility: What if those grants-in-aid were not available? It was generally recognized that Sibley, in adding this pertinent question to the options, revealed the overriding belief among astute observers that private schools would be struck down in federal court. HOPE had been describing the same scenario in their mailings, at chapter meetings and at public forums for months. The organization's leaders took heart that the commission agreed with them and announced their viewpoint to the public. The hearings might be the beginning of the end to this crisis, but no one in HOPE dared predict the outcome.

The first witness at the Americus hearing, Charles F. Crisp, set the tone for the day. Crisp, from an old and powerful political Georgia family and a local bank president, listened intently to Sibley as he described the options, then Crisp announced that all schools in Georgia should be closed rather than to allow Atlanta to proceed with its pupil placement plan. He resisted all arguments from the chairman, stating that the Atlanta plan was a "snare and a delusion: a subterfuge. Like a little integration ... it's only a foot in the door."[4]

Most of the witnesses gave their own opinions but there were groups who presented poll numbers and results from their meetings prior to the hearing. "One Columbus radio station delivered an editorial telling listeners that the school question could not be decided by the Atlanta press, HOPE, or Big Johnny Reb."[5] The station asked their listeners to send in a postcard stating their preference for segregation at any cost or education at any cost. Of twelve hundred responses, 1,192 were for segregation. The commission was witnessing the classic political battle in Georgia that had been going on since Reconstruction: rural and small-town Georgia south of Atlanta against big-city interests. The Black Belt hard-liners speaking in Americus showed how effective their politicians had been in convincing them there were legitimate ways to keep schools segregated in Georgia.

Only one voice pleaded for local option in the morning session. Mrs. Robert Robinson of the Marion County PTA explained her county was too poor to convert to private schools and relied on state funding.

Americus priest Father Finian Riley in the afternoon made an eloquent appeal for local option or secret ballot to decide the issue. But perhaps his most salient contribution was to remind the commission and those in attendance the role that intimidation plays in speaking out on the school issue: "That for someone to speak out publicly, for any type of integration, is to invite recriminations, social, economic, and even physical."[6]

Sibley had prepared questions to ask black witnesses, drawing on a speech made by the black preacher, the Reverend R. W. Greene, after the *Brown* decision. Greene had cited the reasons why blacks preferred a segregated school system: the employment of many blacks, the fostering of leadership skills among their own people, and the value of black teachers instructing black students. He also gave the state credit for a growing equality in the segregated school system. The chairman gave free rein to the Rev. Greene on the witness stand and he was not disappointed. Greene assured the audience that blacks wanted segregated schools.[7]

The next witness, a tall, lanky, well-dressed black man, was a retired principal, who scratched his head, as he looked at the chairman and said, "Mr. Sibley, to answer your question about won't separate but equal schools work, I don't think so. It's like a one-legged man who goes into the shoe store. They don't let him buy just one shoe. He has to buy a pair of shoes. Well sir, we've done wore out the separate, and we ain't even tried on the equal."[8] Now it was time for the chairman to scratch his head as laughter filled the courtroom.

The day ended with black delegations from Sumter, Stewart, and

Chattahoochee counties, all of whom favored segregation. One delegate spoke of the "good will and present friendship that exists between our races. We are happy."[9] The crowd applauded.

Frances Pauley watched in admiration while Armine Dimon testified to a largely hostile audience, explaining, "I don't believe what it appears that the general public believes. I think that we should have desegregated schools, and it will not ruin our school system."[10] Pauley knew it required amazing courage for Dimon, a white woman, to stand up against her community in South Georgia.

The testimony of blacks at the Americus hearing drew positive response from the segregationists in South Georgia. Marvin Griffin praised the witnesses for having "more sense than the folks in HOPE ... or the agitators in the NAACP ... [and] the Supreme Court of the United States."[11]

Some white people were upset over the use of black testimony. One of John Greer's senatorial colleagues came up to him and asked, "What's all these niggers doing in here?" Greer answered that blacks were here to testify. The legislator replied, "Well, that ain't the way I understood it. I thought we were just going around the state and let the whites talk it over, decide what we'd do and then we'd tell the niggers about it."[12]

Sixty-six people testified in Americus. Fifty-two, representing groups whose membership exceeded 12,500, preferred closing the schools. The five proponents of the second option represented twenty-three people. Nine blacks testified, and all but one favored continuing segregation. The state's NAACP issued a protest statement, claiming that the blacks had been pressured by local white school administrators to voice a preference for segregation.

Sibley came away from Americus stunned to find the white people in South Georgia so rigidly unshakable in their commitment to massive resistance. He expected them to be resistant, but the degree of their repugnance to changing their segregated way of life became a valuable lesson for the chairman.

The reaction in Americus did not surprise Betty Harris, who was in the audience. The controversial Koinonia, a farm community started in 1942 in Americus as an interracial Christian "commune," had infuriated the local population since its beginning. Harris knew Koinonia well and supported its mission. The violent opposition to the interracial project had only increased over the years.[13] The Sibley hearings were a chance for whites to express their emotional outrage at what they considered more assaults on their way of life.

After hearing the strong support for massive resistance at the Americus hearing where no one from HOPE was called to testify, Frances Pauley knew her suspicions had been correct. The hurried hearing schedule kept open-school advocates from organizing a strong presence at the hearings. Pauley met with John Sibley and asked him to "play fair." She complained that HOPE was kept from testifying in Americus and to rectify this omission she petitioned for an additional sub-committee hearing in Columbus to allow residents of the third district's only large city to testify. Pauley told the chairman that HOPE was not asking for special treatment, only "justice."[14] After Americus, some HOPE leaders joined Pauley in their belief that the Sibley Commission hearings would be merely a supplement to massive resistance, not a change in policy.

HOPE found the hearings produced a surprise plus for their cause. Television cameras on the witnesses sharply contrasted open-school advocates from resisters. The national media had been on the Georgia story for months and during the Sibley hearings their coverage intensified. The camera showed it all, said one volunteer: "It got so when you saw somebody come up on stage, you'd know whether they were segregationist or not ... they were not actors. They were real ... the people on our side were just so nice ... in comparison with others who were filled with hatred.... It came across on TV."[15]

Atlanta's WSB-TV sent a cameraman, Joe Fain, to every hearing and other stations broadcasted a few hearings live. Radio covered the hearings from gavel to gavel and were the means by which large numbers of the population learned of the day's events. Sometimes television reporters helped to shape the opinions of their audience. Fain's reporting on the day's events aired not only on the local NBC affiliate but also on NBC's nightly news. Fain's camera provided only three to eight minutes of continuous filming, so he "created" news to fill in the gaps. By his own hunch, he filmed testimony he deemed to be most interesting or newsworthy and at times asked a particularly "good" witness to give his testimony in front of the camera after the morning or afternoon session. He drove back to Atlanta in time for his work to appear on the six o'clock news.[16]

By the fourth hearing in La Grange, Georgia, Chairman Sibley realized that the pupil placement plan was unpopular with white Georgians, which prompted him to change strategy. Critics of the commission had to admit that the chairman conducted fair and courteous hearings. Sibley's patrician manner with frequent homespun humor thrown in was accompanied by a quick and facile mind, the very traits that made him an excellent lawyer. The chairman began to relieve anxiety in the crowd by stating there was little chance their communities would face lawsuits if they adopted the local option plan. Their schools could operate as they always had. The status quo could be maintained. This approach was to calm the fears of whites and to separate segregation from resistance.

Part of Sibley's statement at each hearing included his reasons for asking black witnesses different questions from white participants: "So the question that I am asking them [Negroes], and asking them to speak their minds, and speak their hearts — because their children are wrapped up in this very serious and grave question — I am asking them ... in all honesty: would you rather have your schools with your teachers, or had you rather have mixed schools? Now that is the fairest question I can ask them."[17]

Sibley added that if black witnesses preferred to answer only one of the two options he would be glad to honor that request.

The chairman was a perfect example of how the patrician southern white man had been dealing with blacks since Reconstruction. "I will treat you with kindness as long as you realize I know what is best for you." Sibley assumed that "negroes" wanted to keep their schools segregated, an opinion that fit neatly into his strategy of placating whites in their fears of integration. He also banked on the recent upgrading of schools for blacks in the state since the *Brown* decision. New school buildings had been built in rural areas, new buses provided and many black teachers were employed. Why would they want to send their children to white schools when their facilities had markedly improved? This simplistic, naïve credo in the tenets of white paternalism clouded Chairman Sibley's expectations of the hearings.

If the commission could gain support for local option with rural whites, the chairman found it worth the risk to expose potential black discontent. But just as the white boss took offense if his black workers talked back, Sibley began to portray blacks who favored integration as malcontents and not representative of the larger African-American community.

The chairman's strategy seemed to work during the morning session in La Grange. Most of the witnesses spoke for open schools. Seventeen out of 23 witnesses preferred local option. It looked as if Troup County and other counties in the Fourth Congressional District were convinced they could decide the fate of their schools without fear of lawsuit.

Segregationists rallied around their cause in the afternoon, bringing about a reversal to the morning's outcome. Witnesses represented rural organizations, including white supremacy groups, farm bureaus, Lions Clubs, veterans associations and other male-dominated organizations. They all expressed an intense aversion to changing state law that would allow any desegregation. One witness put it this way: "Private schools would start bad and get better by the month. Total integration would start not so bad and get worse forever." Another man said he was willing to have his two granddaughters "grow up ignorant" rather than permit integration. A northerner testified that if Georgia adopted a pupil placement law (which he described as a "method of surrendering"), all the Yankees in the state would move back north.[18]

The La Grange meeting ended with forty-seven people testifying they would prefer changing state law and forty-one preferring continued resistance.

Often the chairman and some of the commission members stayed overnight in a hotel after a day's hearing to cut down on their driving time. Also, the winter-like weather made roads hazardous. At the end of the day over drinks before dinner, it was a time to unwind, to discard their official roles and to talk openly about the day's events. Some spoke of their astonishment at the numbers that came out in the icy conditions. They talked about witnesses, television and newspaper reporters, especially ones who irked them, and they could be heard laughing at times. The men admired John Sibley for his intellectual grasp of the facts and his ability to speak to witnesses from every background with respect and with a sense of humor when needed. They also knew from television reports and from newspapers that he and the commission were taking a beating from the segregationist politicians. Their vitriolic attacks centered on how the panel was just a scheme to force race-mixing.[19]

The national television coverage of the Sibley Commission hearings created great interest across the country, prompting many Americans to write John Sibley. One California woman wrote, "Ever since the public hearings broadcast over TV, I feel constrained to voice my own opinions in behalf of the South." A Tennessee man congratulated Sibley on the "dignified and courteous manner [he] treated every witness regardless of color."[20]

The hot glare of television lights made some witnesses nervous and tongue-tied. Harold Boggs, mayor of Danielsville and Madison County's representative to the Georgia general assembly, became so overwhelmed that he loudly proclaimed he was "for integration 100 percent, regardless of cost." Sibley suggested he think that statement over. To which Boggs replied, "Segregation, Segregation, Segregation," having realized his mistake. Sibley, turning to the members of the press, asked them, "For the sake of the gentleman's political future, please correct that into the record."[21]

Chapter 10

No Stone Unturned

There must be nothing more painful for a man than an undelivered speech.[1]

— John Sibley

Sibley changed his normal opening statement as he spoke to the seven hundred citizens gathered at the Douglas High School gymnasium in Douglas County. He assured his audience that if most communities in Georgia agreed to voluntary segregation and used ideas of the second option, they would not have to integrate their schools. He insinuated that the commission's recommendation would reflect the strong diversity of opinion in the state. He believed it best for each community to work out its problems and if black and white citizens "prefer their own schools we don't have a substantial issue and the matter can work itself out without letting the law take charge of our schools.... The white people and the colored people can settle this question outside the law if they want to settle it."[2]

The fifth hearing was held in the town of Douglas, which represented the Eighth Congressional District in the extreme southeastern part of the state where tobacco and timber ruled the landscape. The district encompassed two large towns, Valdosta in Lowndes County and Brunswick in Glynn County. The hard-line resisters made their most dramatic stand so far at the Douglas hearing. They led entire county delegations to the stand to voice their opinion to close schools rather than submit to any shape or form of desegregation. Many organizations sent representatives to announce results of their polls showing unanimous support of defiance. Previous hearings gave the impression that the resisters only represented themselves while witnesses in favor of the second option spoke for organizations with many more citizens. The press so far had given an inaccurate portrayal of the sentiment of the hearings. They failed to report that if all resisters had registered at the hearings, they would have outnumbered those in favor of the second option by a considerable margin.

The commission heard 148 witnesses in five hours in the town of Douglas. As the threat of integration escalated, the Ku Klux Klan and white Citizens Councils made inroads into many Georgia communities. The scare tactic worked with the "high and mighty" and the most vulnerable whites. The scene harkened back to the days of Eugene Talmadge and his machine that dominated Georgia politics for so many decades. A likeminded Valdosta delegation led by John Langdale, patriarch of a prominent and powerful family, approached the podium to record an "amen" to continued resistance. In his effort to present a united front, he used his position with the county PTA to block representatives from the Salles-Mahone Elementary School from appearing before the commission to announce the results of a poll showing a preference for open schools.[3]

County commissioners from across the state met in Augusta that March and voted to uphold segregation laws. Roy Harris, their spokesman, accused the Sibley Commission of muddling the issue and spreading "confusion" and warned that "if Atlanta desegregates its schools, the NAACP, backed up by the federal government and all the money in the world [will] move in against your little county ... [and] ram race-mixing down your throats."

Harris led the effort to ensure that alternatives to open schools would be heard at the final meetings. Members of the Klu Klux Klan and States' Rights and Citizens Councils held rallies the night before a scheduled meeting with many attempting to coerce PTA organizations either to stay home or to state a preference for segregation. The Klu Klux Klan held a gigantic statewide cross burning one Saturday night. The Metropolitan Association for Segregated Education (MASE) sent a form letter to supporters urging them to overwhelm the Sibley Commission with letters of support for resistance.

"Dominos." *Atlanta Constitution*, 1960. Clifford H. "Baldy" Baldowski Editorial Cartoons. Courtesy of the Richard B. Russell Library for Political Research and Studies, University of Georgia Libraries.

From the first hearing in Americus, Chairman John Sibley had been trying to separate the school question from segregation, but it had little effect on witnesses. One after another came to the stand and just said "segregation" and sat down. But the interesting fact was that many came into the hearing all pumped up, thinking, "Man, I'm gonna give my speech and we're gonna stop this thing dead in its tracks," and the next day the resister began to step back a bit, think about the voices heard at the hearing and wonder if maybe he was as die-hard as he thought. The public's furor over the schools died down after the hearing in each district. Permitting the people to vent their anger in a controlled setting with a skilled, likable and courteous chairman seemed to verify the predictions by those who believed the governor had manifested a stroke of genius when he appointed John Sibley. Frances Pauley and other HOPE leaders were too much in the thick of things to evaluate Sibley or the hearings. They worked day and night to find suitable witnesses and prepare them to testify at the rest of the hearings.

In the middle of the month of hearings, newspapers and television ran stories of lunch counter sit-ins by black students in Atlanta and other protests being staged in Savannah. Governor Vandiver responded to the sit-ins true to form, asserting that these protests were the work of communists "calculated to breed dissatisfaction, discomfort, discord and evil."[4]

These demonstrations did not enhance Sibley's arguments that blacks preferred their own schools nor segregation in the larger sense. If blacks wanted to sit at white lunch counters, then a natural conclusion would be that blacks also want to attend white schools. The sit-ins were not popular with Atlanta's black leaders who had orchestrated every improvement in the community and were offended by college kids acting on their own. The leaders were solidly behind the *Calhoun v. Latimer* suit. They did not see how these protests would help the cause.

At the Sandersville hearing in Washington County in the Sixth Congressional District, witnesses expressed their overall view of changes coming to the South as had been pointed out by the sit-ins. Support for the status quo was the order of the day with white churches getting on the resister bandwagon. A witness representing the Washington County Ministerial Association read a statement claiming, "The present system is best for the Southland.... We deplore the work of agitators which have stirred up our people.... We say abolish the public schools rather than accept any degree of integration."[5]

Emory C. Gilbert, a member of the Georgia general assembly, irritated the chairman by sparring with him "over the commission's potential scenario of continued resistance and Sibley's disparaging remarks toward a conversion to private schools."[6]

The chairman had discouraged legislators from testifying at their county hearings, because the panel was created to hear from ordinary citizens, not officials. Sibley did not want the voices of assemblymen opposed to option two to be overemphasized.

Once again, the split between the city or sizable town and country was apparent from Bibb County representatives. The Macon chapter of HOPE, the Bibb County League of Women Voters and the Macon Civic Women's Club all voted for option two. Businessmen introduced their concerns. If schools closed in the state, the economy would suffer greatly. One woman from Jones County testifying for local option ended her testimony with: "The only possible good that [could] come out of closing the schools is, thank goodness, no more PTA meetings."[7]

The hearing in Sylvania again demonstrated the wide divide between town and country. W. W. Law of the Chatham County NAACP temporarily interrupted the boycott he was leading in Savannah to lead a delegation to Sylvania. The fourteen members of the group walked down from the courthouse's segregated balcony en masse and stood in front of the podium waiting to be heard. Law said to Sibley:

> "I speak not only for the thousands of colored members [of the NAACP] of Georgia, but for the thousands ... of Negroes and whites who are victims of intimidation. These men and women are silent because they dare not say what is really and truly in their hearts. I even speak for the Negro teachers who were brought before this committee and required to answer questions as to their positions in regard to the maintenance of segregation as the best thing for public schools, in the presence of their white superiors and superintendents who insist [on] segregation."[8]

He then asked Sibley, "What other position do you expect these Negro teachers to take?" Law demanded an immediate end to segregation "to guarantee the same educational opportunities for white and Negro youths."

As Law spoke from the podium, people began to murmur and by the end of his statement the crowd erupted into cries of indignation. Sibley, clearly annoyed by Law's testimony, asked if the NAACP had groomed these black witnesses. Law denied the accusation. The chairman asked Law if he spoke for all the black witnesses in the courtroom, some of whom had earlier testified in favor of segregation. He told Law to take a seat and said he would poll the Chatham County delegation himself.

The next witness, Hosea Williams, represented the Morris Brown Alumni Association and the Butler Presbyterian Church. He told Sibley he took the same position, saying, "The poor thing about the hearings — the citizens of Georgia were not given —." Sibley cut him off in mid-sentence and asked him: "What do you want?" to which Williams replied, "I want integration." The twelve remaining members of the NAACP delegation, except two, insisted that nothing less that immediate integration would be satisfactory. The audience booed the NAACP members and other open-school advocates. Sibley rapped the gavel for order repeatedly. He told the Sylvania gathering that there had been a little disorder at other hearings but none like this and he lamented that witnesses could not be heard with all the commotion. "Let's not destroy the spirit of this meeting."[9]

Thereafter the commission heard from open-school advocates, representing the Savannah chapter of the League of Women Voters, HOPE, B'nai B'rith, the local chapter of American Association of University Women and several ministerial and PTA groups. So far, Chatham was the only county to show sizable support for the second commission option.

At the March 21st hearing in Moultrie all fourteen counties in this district registered a majority of witnesses for option one. Many important political leaders spoke or groomed their delegations to testify against open schools. Most of these Democrats had joined a motorcade they had organized through the local newspaper, leaving the town of Bainbridge at 8:30 in the morning for Moultrie. All district representatives to the General Assembly had signed a manifesto the previous month vowing to maintain state laws. George Busbee, sponsor of the bill that created the Sibley Commission, attended the hearing and told the press the local option plan was "hogwash" and a "diversionary tactic."[10]

Organizations from the larger cities in the district, Tifton, Thomasville and Albany, however, registered support for the second option. The *Albany Herald* also encouraged its readers to testify but advised them that Georgia's only real choices were segregation and tuition grants. An Emory University student, Shirley Freeman, scoffed at the idea of private schools: "You also know that these politicians who tell you that you can have private schools for your children have no plan." She admonished the crowd, "They say private schools, fine, everything is going to work out all right, but they have no plan; and you should also know that most of you cannot afford private schools because you don't have the money."[11]

Freeman's testimony could have come right out of HOPE's manual. The private school fantasy, first denounced by representative Muggsy Smith in his Spring Street School speech in 1958, had at last found a larger platform.

Supporters of segregation at any cost still held the day, drowning out open-school advocates. Rabid segregationists made their final stand in Moultrie. While politicians guided constituents through their testimonies here, another state politician, James Mackay of Dekalb County, released a statement to the press in which he outlined a possible death knoll to massive resistance legislation in the assembly. Mackay made the argument that if the decision that no state could deny funding to a school solely on the basis of integration was challenged in a higher court, this procedure would cause the General Assembly to decide the issue. He presented the following scenario: An Atlanta school would be integrated, then the governor would close the school and cut off its funding, parents of affected schoolchildren would file suit to reopen the school, the court would then order funding restored and declare the state's mandatory school closing laws invalid. The legislature would then be forced into restoring schools funds to the integrated school or vote to eliminate funding to all Georgia schools. Mackay (a longtime open-school advocate) believed strongly that the General Assembly would never pass a statewide school closing bill. Although the legislators would sacrifice Atlanta's schools and even the entire state's education system — if the court ordered them closed — most could not bear the responsibility of voting to close the schools themselves.[12] Although Mackay's school closing scenario must have been partly aimed at the federal judges confronting Georgia's resistance laws, the Dekalb County representative's idea of forcing the General Assembly to vote to abandon public schools, he hoped to influence the fast approaching final battle over desegregation in the legislature.

The Fifth Congressional District hearing in Atlanta was billed as the hearing to watch. A week before the Atlanta hearing, the press geared up the public for what they predicted would be a battle between HOPE and MASE. The president of the segregationist group, T. J. Wesley, Jr., sent letters to members and supporters urging them to attend the meeting. Wesley wanted his people to give their views and not let the integrationists like Ralph McGill of the *Atlanta Constitution,* and the mayor, Mr. Hartsfield, "who arrogate unto themselves a monopoly on wisdom and virtue and the prerogative of being spokesmen for all the people."[13] HOPE leaders knew they had to make their strongest stand in the capital city. They made their selections carefully with special emphasis on mothers of school-age children, most of whom were not publicly affiliated with the open-schools movement.

The editorial pages of Atlanta newspapers lauded the wisdom of the local option plan. This public endorsement was one of the Sibley Commission's most important achievements. The *Calhoun Times* pointed out that the diversity of opinion demonstrated at the hearings proved the need for local choice. Other writers suggested deciding the issue by secret ballot. A Waycross editor agreed that a referendum was necessary for the rank and file of plain people to express their views. He warned that the hearings had changed and become forums for "extremists and professional agitators."[14]

On the morning of the twenty-third of March, with school let out for the day, Atlanta police officers guided witnesses to the parking lot of Henry Grady High School before opening the doors of the gymnasium. A bald man stood at the entrance to the gym handing out handbills that featured a black man and white woman dancing together with the caption: "Do you want this to happen in Georgia?" The man represented U.S. Klans and was removed from the school property.

The city had prepared for any eventuality of the day by making sure there were uniformed policemen scattered throughout the crowd. Georgia Bureau of Investigation plainclothesmen milled among the people. The Commission was seated behind an elevated table at one end of the basketball court. It was hard to see them over the bank of television and movie cameras. TV reporters from all over the country were in attendance and one local station broadcast the hearing live. Over a thousand people sat on bleachers and folding chairs set up on the gym floor.

John Sibley called the hearing to order a few minutes after ten o'clock. He asked the audience to maintain their decorum throughout the day, explaining that his daughter had just given him a gavel and to please cooperate lest he break his gift.

As expected, Atlanta witnesses gave an enthusiastic endorsement to the local option plan. Eighty-five of 114 witnesses, most representing some Atlanta group or organization, testified they preferred changing state law to accommodate local option and the Atlanta plan. Some of the city's most distinguished leaders, including those from the black community, school systems and churches spoke in favor of self-determination. Finally, the Atlanta Chamber of Commerce got on board and endorsed the local option plan.

The first witness, A. C. Latimer, president of the Atlanta school board and defendant of the school desegregation suit, gave the background on the school issue in Atlanta, explaining how the desegregation plan would work, emphasizing that the city's geographical segregation will limit the mixing of the races. He pointed out the extreme difficulty Atlanta would have if the state converted to private schools: "the city could hardly be expected to make adequate provisions for Atlanta's one hundred thousand school-aged children."[15]

Fran Breeden testified as the mother of four school-age children and as chairperson of HOPE.[16] Judy Neiman, an active Atlanta HOPE volunteer, had come to the city from Chicago and a career in advertising. A smartly dressed, sophisticated woman who was a natural public speaker, Neiman told the commission that as a mother, she believed public education was necessary to a democracy. John Pendergrast, Nan's sixteen-year-old son, testified in favor of desegregation as a high school senior. Nan's beloved fifth-grade teacher came up to her after the hearing and asked, "How could you let your son speak like that?" It was a terribly disappointing blow to Nan, especially coming from a person whom she had admired from childhood.[17]

Other HOPE supporters spoke for local option, representing PTA organizations, Women's Clubs, Georgia League of Woman Voters and church groups.

The opposition to local option was heard in the morning session as MASE's president, T. J. Wesley, Jr., said that some people's priorities were skewed. "Some of our people are saying, save our schools. We say, save our children first." He went on to describe how conversion to private schools might work, including public auctions of school properties and supplies to private individuals. An official of the U.S. Klans spoke for maintaining state law as well as other persons who testified for the same position.[18]

The afternoon session sizzled with conflict. One man, a descendent of Stonewall Jackson, claimed that if his grandfather had heard "the testimony of some of our people here this morning he would have us shot at sunrise as traitors." Later, a woman who claimed she was a descendent of Civil War veterans, spoke in favor of local option not on behalf of her grandfathers but for her children. Lester Maddox, the very vocal opponent to open schools and especially critical of HOPE, urged the crowd to fight against communists and integrationists who were creating the "greatest tragedy occurring in America." On the same note, Mrs. May Andrews stated that integration "leads to the Communist goals of amalgamation of the races [and] promotes centralization of power and uses the Negro to set up a police state with the federal government policing the situation."[19] Loud cheers and clapping came from the resisters answered by vociferous boos from the other side. The chairman pounded his gavel over and over to quiet the gathering and said he would move the hearing to a classroom away from the shouting and hollering if it didn't stop.

The meeting ended with some of the city's most esteemed black leaders speaking in agreement with local option. These men had a long history of working with Atlanta's white establishment, which had produced advancements for blacks, such as convincing Mayor Hartsfield to hire blacks on the police force. Donald Hollowell, one of the Atlanta attorneys representing the plaintiffs in *Calhoun v. Latimer*, read his statement.

"We, the ten parents who filed the suit against the Atlanta Board of Education want you to know why we did it. Our children never got, they don't get now and we don't believe they will ever get equal education under a separate system. Therefore, the only thing to do is to do away with segregation like the Supreme Court said to do. Then all children, white and colored, will get the same education."[20]

The Ninth Congressional District hearing occurred in Gainesville, Georgia, on March 24, the last scheduled meeting. As most predicted, a large majority in the Ninth Congressional District favored local option. The negative effects closing schools would have on business was a major theme of the day. A low black population in the district brought forth fewer dissenters to option two. Only Jackson and Barrow counties with large farming operations produced any sizable outcry of resisters.

The intense lobbying effort spearheaded by Frances Pauley of HOPE paid off when John Sibley scheduled a subcommittee hearing in Columbus, Georgia, on March 31 to rectify the inadequate representation of the city at the Americus hearing. Pauley and other HOPE leaders were furious over the lopsided results in Americus, realizing that to be fair the commission needed to hear from witnesses from the only large city in the Third Congressional District. HOPE knew there were many open-school advocates waiting to be heard. Acting chairman John Duncan presided at the meeting. John Sibley was back in Atlanta conducting a second day of hearings for those individuals who were waiting to be heard when time ran out. The commission made sure it was viewed as an impartial body, flexible enough to change its schedule to hear from all the people.

The Columbus hearing followed the pattern of a rural-urban split of opinion. The usual groups from church and school groups and women's organizations testified for local option. The big victory for open-school advocates came when the Columbus Chamber of Commerce joined its Atlanta colleagues and supported open schools. Local Machinists Union, the Columbus Association of Master Barbers, and Citizens Councils and the U.S. Knights of the Ku Klux Klan all believed fervently in keeping segregation in Georgia at any cost.

Columbus boasted they had the largest contingent of black witnesses at any of the hearings, with a group of seventy-five people giving support to the seventeen that testified. All but one of the black witnesses spoke in favor of option two. R. W. Greene, who testified at the Americus hearing and had attended all the hearings, came out again for segregation of the schools. But this time he was booed by black witnesses.[21]

John Sibley's patience wore thin by the time of the second Atlanta hearing. He cut into long-winded witnesses and asked them to state their preference and sit down. Some refused and continued talking until Sibley, in exasperation, rapped the gavel, interrupting them in mid-sentence, to state their time was up, please sit down. Seventy-one people chose option two and forty-nine opposed that view in the second Atlanta hearing.

During the month of March, the Sibley Commission heard from more than 1,600 witnesses from 148 of the state's 159 counties. Although Sibley's composure had been sorely tested throughout the proceedings, he maintained his friendly manner, sometimes exchanging banter and jokes with witnesses and intently listening to them. With those who seemed close to his age, he admonished them to not brag about their grandchildren unless they had more than his eleven. His calm, firm control of the hearings and his patriarchal presence were reasons why the General Assembly Committee on Schools became known as the Sibley Commission.

Women had gathered in Muriel Lokey's living room one and a half years earlier to challenge the silence that surrounded the impending school crisis. HOPE was born to break that silence and to do all it could to keep public schools open. The first goal had been accomplished. The Sibley hearings made it politically and socially acceptable to talk openly about segregation, desegregation, local option, and private school plans. And in many respects HOPE had made these hearings feasible. The people had awakened to the real possibility that their schools might be closed. HOPE volunteers could take pride in their work, so far but the final outcome was very much in doubt. These women who had put in countless hours of their time to move the school crisis to the forefront of the Georgia mind knew in their hearts that the battle of Atlanta held the final linchpin to the success or failure of the open-school movement.

John Sibley left no stone unturned. Before the hearings began, he sent lawyers out to other southern states to see if there were ways to con-

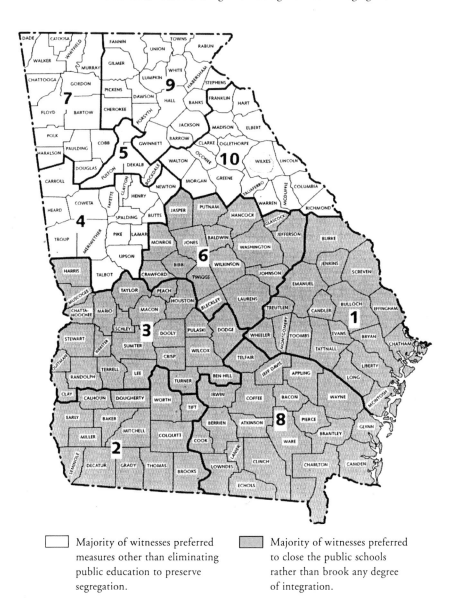

| | Majority of witnesses preferred measures other than eliminating public education to preserve segregation. | | Majority of witnesses preferred to close the public schools rather than brook any degree of integration. |

Testimony before the Sibley Commission by congressional district in Georgia, 1960. From *Restructured Resistance* by Jeff Roche, 1998. Courtesy of the University of Georgia Press.

tain desegregation, unknown to Georgia lawmakers. The information gathered from these investigations formed the structure of an amendment included in the commission's final majority report to the General Assembly.[22]

The Sibley Commission had made it possible for the people of Georgia to participate in a statewide town meeting to determine the fate of their public schools. The hearings revealed a profound clash between the culture of the old South and modern America. It was political drama that few Americans experienced first-hand. It was democracy in action.

Chapter 11

Operation Last Chance

If the schools close, then students and teachers may suffer, but that responsibility will be with the Georgia Legislature.[1]

— Constance Baker Motley

Lucy Huie, a housewife and mother, lived twenty miles north of Atlanta in Jonesboro, the site of a famous Civil War battle that preceded the defeat of Atlanta in 1864. Nearly a hundred years later there were many Jonesboro residents who were still tied emotionally to the southern cause, even if it meant closing the schools. Huie was not one of them. She could not imagine her children without a school to attend. She was a stay-at-home mother who led her daughter's scout troop, baked cookies for PTA receptions and furnished transportation for school events. As the school crisis unfolded, an Atlanta friend called Huie and asked her to form a HOPE chapter. She agreed to do so, starting with the mothers of her Girl Scout troop. At the close of a HOPE meeting held at a local church one night, Huie and her husband were starting to leave when a woman came running back inside the church screaming, "The Klan is gathering outside. I hope I make it home." They looked out a window and saw three carloads of men wearing pointed hats and robes. Huie could only think about her four children left at home. They had to get out of there. She put on the white gloves that she always carried with her, knowing how the Klan felt about southern womanhood. There was an eerie silence as she and her husband walked through a column of ten or more Klansmen standing in front of their car. Just as they approached the vehicle, the men moved away. Lucy, afraid her husband might start a fight with them, pushed him inside the driver's seat. As the Huies drove away, they could see the men following them from their rear-view mirror. They drove the six blocks to their home with the Klan close behind. On entering the house, the besieged couple spoke quietly to their children, turned the lights out and watched as the men got out of the cars and stood together as though they were having a meeting. Then they drove off. The next week a cross was burned on a bank in front of the Huie house. Thereafter, Huie held HOPE meetings at the courthouse with police protection in mind.[2]

As soon as John Sibley announced there would be a subcommittee hearing in Columbus, Betty Harris organized supporters of open schools in and outside Columbus to testify at the hearing. Lucy Huie agreed to organize two cars of HOPE supporters to drive down to Columbus. The women were seen on television news that night testifying for open schools. The next day the Klansmen burned crosses at the homes of those who appeared at the Columbus hearing. A cross burning on Huie's lawn was nothing new; she could even laugh at the pitifully small crosses. But she became angry when she heard the scared voices of the other women as they told her of their first experience with the Klan. Jonesboro HOPE volunteers were subjected to insults shouted to them on the telephone, in the grocery store and on the street.

Lucy Huie learned about the Ku Klux Klan at age five when her minister father, a Methodist circuit rider in North Georgia, took his family to Sunday dinner at a parishioner's home. There Huie found a white Klan robe hanging in the master bedroom and when asked about it, the adults clammed up. But until her involvement with HOPE, Huie had not realized the extent of the Klan's numbers or influence in Clayton County. She decided to save the cross that burned on a hill opposite her house.[3] She noted that the plywood cross had been wrapped in burlap with the smell of kerosene still pungent.

The Sibley hearings concluded at the end of March, but much important work still awaited the Sibley Commission members. They were expected to turn in their report and recommendations to the governor and assembly as soon as possible. John Sibley insisted their first two meetings be secret to ensure privacy. Their discussions throughout the sessions revealed sharp divisions in how to proceed from this point on. Representatives from the General Assembly on the panel who were for continued resistance to desegregation all along, felt the hearings proved that most Georgians agreed with them. But the majority of the committee members favored changing state law to avoid closing schools. Both parties agreed to submit majority and minority reports with their recommendations to the assembly and to the governor.[4]

On April 28, 1960, John Sibley walked alone into a packed State Supreme Court chamber, sat down at the head of a long table, and placed the majority report of the Committee on Schools in front of him. Commission members filed in and stood around the chairman. Members of the press filled the room. Intense lights of television cameras zeroed in on Sibley, something the chairman had grown accustomed to during the hearings. The chairman read the majority report in his unhurried, softly spoken Georgia accent. He pointed out that the strong division of opinions among the people and the commission members showed the complexity of the situation. Maintaining public education, "the bulwark of a democracy," was the overriding principle of the majority report. Although the chairman made clear the majority disagreed with the *Brown* decision, he warned that the decision "is binding on the lower courts and that it will be enforced."

The majority report, in an effort not to alienate the population with their recommendations, stated their belief that most citizens "prefer taxsupported, segregated schools ... for the peace, good order and tranquility of the state." The report shot down the private school option by claiming it was unworkable and impracticable with huge costs to the state and its citizens.

Chairman Sibley outlined a plan to preserve segregation while not breaking federal law. He maintained most Georgia communities would not be faced with suits to desegregate their schools. Voluntary segregation was the answer for most of Georgia. The thinking went this way: if communities voted to maintain segregated schools, they would not be affected if massive resistance laws were overturned.

The majority report recommended a "freedom of association" amendment to the state constitution that guaranteed each student the right to transfer schools or receive from the state a tuition credit for a private school if his or her school were forced to integrate. A second amendment would offer each community an opportunity to choose for itself through a local election what to do when faced with possible desegregation. Ten men serving on the commission agreed with the chairman and signed the majority report.[5]

A sizable number on the panel disagreed with the chairman and submitted a minority report, calling for the continuation of massive resistance as the majority of people had requested at the hearings. John Duncan, the committee vice-chairman, and the arch-segregationist Peter Zack Geer, wrote the minority opinion. The report argued that the pupil placement plan could not work and that statewide closings were not preordained. The report called for an end to agitation for desegregation by "communist-inspired organizations" [like HOPE], before they inflicted "incalculable damage." The minority recommended that an amendment to the state constitution be enacted that would "guarantee that no Georgia child shall be forced ... to attend any public school wherein a child of the opposite race is enrolled."[6]

A member of the minority, Render Hill, released a separate statement to explain that the division in Georgia was so close, the narrow margin of 55 percent to 45 percent split in opinion, that it required the state to look at other options. He implored those incoming members to the assembly to study the problem and to determine the wishes of their county and to present these at the 1961 session. He challenged the legislature to propose a plan that would "resolve the issues."

The report hit Georgia like a tornado. This was the first time a state-government-sanctioned body advocated overturning massive resistance laws and accepting that desegregation was inevitable. With the results showing sharp division within the state, Governor Vandiver, who had commissioned this endeavor to find out public opinion, found himself in a state of paralysis. It was a politician's nightmare. He refused to call a special session on the matter, convinced it would be "fruitless." He, like most members of the assembly, refused to comment on the commission reports, only praising the members for their efforts.[7]

A few days after the Sibley Commission report was released, Judge Hooper made his ruling on May 9 to a request by the plaintiffs in the *Calhoun v. Latimer* case that he implement his decision to desegregate Atlanta schools by the fall semester of 1960. He noted that public sentiment was changing swiftly in the state. The judge pointed out that the Sibley Commission reported Georgia's citizens voted 3–2 against integration. He said if a poll had been taken a year before, the count would have been 5–0 with no chance for "give."[8]

He denied the plaintiffs' request and charged the General Assembly to take the advice outlined in the commission's majority report and overturn the massive resistance laws. For the first time he gave a flat compliance date of May 1, 1961 as the time when Atlanta schools must put their desegregation plan into action. The judge set May 1 to May 15, 1961 as the period in which applications would be accepted for transfer to white high schools for the 1961 fall semester. Due to the delay in the desegregation process, he modified the plan, adding the 11th grade to the 12th grades to be desegregated in May 1961. The black attorneys for the plaintiffs said at first they would appeal the order but after a conference with Judge Hooper, decided against it.

Judge Hooper made a revealing off-the-cuff statement after announcing a compliance date. He said the new order was not contingent on what action or inaction the 1961 General Assembly might take. The order would go into effect regardless of decisions made by the legislature.[9]

The Atlanta Constitution reported that Atlanta officials were pleased that Judge Hooper's ruling gave them more time to desegregate its schools. A. C. Latimer, chairman of the Atlanta Board of Education, said, "We would hope the General Assembly would pass such laws as will allow us to continue the uninterrupted operation of our schools."

Mayor Hartsfield agreed with Latimer: "I sincerely hope our state leaders and the Legislature will take steps to save public education in our state."

On the same front page of the May 10th edition of the *Constitution* the opposite view was reported: "Top political leaders dashed cold water Monday on hopes that the 1961 General Assembly will enact legislation to avert school closings." James S. Peters, chairman of the State Board of

Education, predicted the issue would have to "be fought out in the primary and general elections." Governor Vandiver said the matter was now in the lap of the 1961 Legislature.

That same spring in 1960, Georgians read and saw on television the foreboding New Orleans situation, which could either entrench their belief that desegregation would not happen in Georgia or the contrary view that the citizens of Georgia must unite against chaos. The federal court had ordered the city schools in New Orleans to desegregate by the following fall semester. The old families of the city had done nothing to avert a crisis, which prompted the mayor to publicly state: "If those SOBs aren't going to do anything, I'll be damned if I'm going to stick my neck out."[10] The New Orleans school board polled parents of school-age children to see if they preferred keeping schools open or closing them. White parents favored closing schools five to one and blacks overwhelmingly supported desegregation. The legislature and its committees were issued constraining orders by the court. The legislature froze the school board's assets, appointed new school boards and urged whites to boycott the schools while the mighty Catholic Church did nothing. New Orleans was finally forced to comply with the desegregation order. They chose two grade schools in working-class neighborhoods to desegregate in the fall of that year.[11]

The floor leaders of the 1959–60 Georgia House and Senate predicted the 1961 assembly would hold the line against desegregating the schools. The state school superintendent, Claude Purcell, who served on the Sibley Commission, "said he sees little chance for a solution until schools have been closed and existing laws tested."[12]

Judge Hooper made his opinion patently clear that the 1961 Assembly had sole power to avert school closings. The judge declared this was their "last chance" to find a solution without chaos.[13]

Representative Frank Twitty, House floor leader, said the opinions of the great majority of legislators would reflect the will of their people. Roy Harris, an arch ally of Twitty, made speeches slamming the commission, its chairman and its majority report. The hard-liners received steady newspaper coverage south of Atlanta. If the old guard from rural counties continued to win assembly seats, then they could still outvote the urban areas under the county unit system. No group knew this better than HOPE. The grass roots organization faced an uphill battle. They called it "Operation Last Chance."

John Sibley was of the same mind. He knew the next seven months were crucial in selling the state on the commission's recommendations. To do this, he and others who sided with the majority accepted speaking engagements throughout the state. Sibley was interviewed by Edward R. Murrow for a documentary entitled, "Who Speaks for the South?" When Murrow returned to Atlanta to finish taping the program, the newscaster made it clear: "This is in no sense an effort to solve the [school] question or agitate on segregation. The only people who will be heard in the documentary will be Georgians." These assurances stemmed apparently from incidents in Nashville where CBS-TV had been accused of causing strife.[14]

In Murrow's interview with Governor Vandiver, the governor refused to give his support to either the majority or minority report, only praising the commission for "doing such a fine job ... they acted in what they believed to be the best interests of this state."[15] In answer to an Atlanta reporter's question, Murrow said he probably would not interview Roy Harris.

As soon as a John Sibley speech given at a Rotarian club or chamber of commerce was reported in the local press, the opposition shot a salvo across the bow of public opinion. Roy Harris, Griffin Bell and other politicians kept up the drumbeat of resistance, maintaining it was the will of the majority in the state. On this point, they were right. In actual numbers, more Georgians favored segregation at any cost. On the flip side, their numbers had gone down during and after the commission hearings, supplying their oratory firepower with heightened fury to not surrender "our way of life" to outsiders — the beginning signs of desperation.

HOPE held a "Georgia Open School Conference" at Atlanta's Dinkler Plaza Hotel following Judge Hooper's May decision. Its purpose was to announce the progress the open-school movement had made to date and to offer participants the opportunity to brainstorm ideas of what to do in the coming months before the January 1961 legislative session. Atlanta state senator Muggsy Smith suggested the group use outdoor advertising throughout southern Georgia with the theme: "Your schools will close too." Mayor Hartsfield recommended HOPE mail a cheap newspaper emphasizing the wisdom of the Sibley proposals to offset Roy Harris's opposition paper, *Augusta Courier*. The most important thrust of the ensuing campaign involved pressuring business leaders and legislators to accept the recommendations of the majority report and overturn massive resistance laws.[16]

HOPE called a special meeting of its board of directors on June 8 at Fran Breeden's home. A financial crisis was looming. Something had to be done to bring in dollars for the vital campaign adopted at the May conference. Operation Last Chance was making big plans for statewide conferences, petitions, newsletters, and advertising across the state. Judy Neiman led the advertising campaign with dramatic HOPE ads in newspapers: Below the face of a child, were big, bold letters: "NOW ... SHALL WE BLIND THESE EYES TO KNOWLEDGE?" Another pungent ad read, ... "They thought they could go it alone, so they closed the public schools in Prince Edward County, Virginia. A PRINCE EDWARD PRIMER — A is for Attic — You wouldn't want your child to shiver up there. B is for Basement — So crowded and dim, No lunches, no busses, not even a gym. C is Curriculum — Sharply curtailed, How costly a lesson — the students all failed!"[17]

HOPE had run on financial optimism from the beginning, relying on donations that trickled into the office, a few substantial amounts but mostly five, ten and twenty-five dollar contributions. The treasury was hitting rock bottom, and with so much work to do, the board decided to conduct a major fund-raising campaign under the direction of a professional fund-raiser. Now that HOPE's efforts to keep schools open had been favorably recognized in the aftermath of the Sibley Commission hearings, the board believed moneyed people and businesses were ready to open their wallets wider to further the work they were beginning to see as vital.

More than fifty people attended HOPE's quarterly open board meeting in October at an Atlanta restaurant. It was a time to review the organization's progress so far and to incorporate ideas from the May conference in making plans for Operation Last Chance. A series of four "Days of Decision" forums, jointly sponsored by HOPE, United Church Women,

"Don't Let It Happen Here." HOPE flyer during Operation Last Chance.
Courtesy of the HOPE/Lokey Papers, Atlanta History Center Archives.

League of Women Voters, and Active Voters of Georgia, would be held around the state in which for the first time influential political leaders would take part. Frances Pauley announced efforts being made to further expand HOPE's statewide organization to form a quick-reaction group ready to respond to anything coming out of the January legislative session. Various sections of the state were assigned to chapters and individuals to accomplish this objective.[18]

Beverly Downing, one of the first organizers of an Athens, Georgia, HOPE chapter and a HOPE board member, believed that business leaders across the state had to be mobilized to put pressure on the political structure as well as make substantial donations for Operation Last Chance. "Money talks. Not the bleeding hearts like us," she told Fran Breeden.[19]

Downing's father, H. Edsel Benson, had run a very successful bakery business in Athens for decades. Benson Fruitcake was his signature product known throughout Georgia. Downing knew her father treated blacks with the same patriarchal condescension of most southerners, but he, with his daughter's input, had begun to realize the certain negative economic fallout in the state if the schools closed. His opinions concerning blacks began to evolve from the old southern school to a more respectful attitude. He agreed to chair a committee of top-flight businessmen across the state to put pressure on the legislature to change state law during their 1961 session to avoid schools closing. Benson used the same method that Downing had adopted in the "country club approach" when she first tried to reach the wider Athens community. Benson convinced a well-respected, successful businessman to sit on the open-schools committee. That person in turn would approach another high-level businessman and so it went. The logic was simple. If a highly respected person approached him, the businessman felt it was a safe move to be included in such company.

During the fall of 1960, Bensen and Downing organized meetings with the newly recruited businessmen to explain the real damage that school closings would have on the state's economy. They were successful in mobilizing 986 leading Georgia businessmen to sign an unequivocal open-schools statement in the form of a telegram to the governor and the legislature at the opening of the session in January 1961.[20]

Before the emergence of the Sibley Commission, Atlanta's business community had been put on notice by Mayor Hartsfield and HOPE as to the disastrous effects of schools closing, which resulted in business leaders organizing meetings and petitions. After the commission majority made its recommendations, Atlanta businessmen were motivated to take a more active role in securing the economic future of the state. John Sibley orchestrated a plan to introduce an open-schools amendment drafted by constitutional attorney Freeman Leverett. Working with Atlanta Chamber of Commerce President Ivan Allen, Jr., Sibley planned to have rural members of the assembly introduce "House Bill number eight" in the next session. By January 1961 there were twenty-eight signatures on the legislation, including the entire delegation from Fulton and Dekalb counties. Atlanta bankers called their trustees who resided across the state to contact their representatives to support the open-schools amendment.[21] The Georgia legislature and big business had always enjoyed a symbiotic relationship. But this fight was different. The wise did not predict the outcome of this one.

On November 11, 1960, Frank Twitty, House floor leader, and Carl Sanders, Senator pro tem, made a joint prediction while in Macon at a pre-legislative forum: "Any proposal to repeal Georgia's school-closing laws at the January-February session of the Legislature will fail." Sanders said the "freedom of choice" plan would not be given consideration until and unless courts strike down existing laws. Twitty and Sanders went on to say, "The Legislature would act to preserve public education after a 'temporary' shutdown."[22]

That fall the country had been exposed to the ongoing battle in New Orleans. As ordered, the city integrated two grade schools in the fall of 1960. "New Orleans provided an epic-length drama more shocking than Little Rock in the intensity of hate it portrayed."[23] White parents pulled their children out of school, protesters were so violent that federal marshals were sent in to escort the four first-grade black students and yet rotten eggs, rocks, debris and obscenities were continually thrown at the children. It was this backdrop of violence in a neighboring state that could keep progressive Atlantans awake at night. The city's future was still in doubt.

A petition to outlaw the NAACP was being circulated among the separate schools faction to the members of the 1961 General Assembly. The petition read in part, "to outlaw the NAACP on the grounds that this organization is of a subversive nature and detrimental to the well being of both races." Quoting Eugene Cook, attorney general of Georgia, "The files of the House on un–American activities committee reveal records of affiliation with or participation in the Communist, Communist Front [organizations] ... on the part of present officials." At the bottom of the petition capital letters read: "YOU EITHER FIGHT NOW FOR YOUR RIGHTS OR SURRENDER TO MOB VIOLENCE AND REVOLUTIONISTS." A signed petition was sent to the HOPE office with an addendum: "HOPE should be outlawed too."[24]

Fran Breeden immediately sent a telegram on behalf of HOPE, to Governor Vandiver, protesting the statements of the floor leaders: "To literally tens of thousands of intelligent Georgians ... this casual prediction of a 'temporary' closing of Georgia's schools indicates that you plan a course of action which is both dangerous and indefensible." She went on to say, "May I respectfully call your attention to the contrast between the states of Arkansas and Virginia where the schools did close temporarily, and North Carolina where no such damaging course was followed." She closed by citing that the Sibley Commission's majority report offered a fair and intelligent solution in which schools could continue to operate without interruption.[25]

The driving force behind convincing assembly members to overturn the massive resistance laws was the belief that Governor Vandiver did not know how to proceed in the school crisis. The Sibley Commission had opened a Pandora's box of an aroused public and a polarized division of opinion. On top of his political troubles, the governor was not in good health, having suffered a heart attack during March. He spent the autumn of 1960 preparing for either eventuality: to oppose the federal government when the fall school year opened in 1961 or, if public sentiment allowed, to overturn resistance laws in the next assembly. To save his political life, the governor had been vying for an appointment as Secretary of the Army with the upcoming Kennedy administration, having helped the presidential candidate win Georgia's electoral votes. He also had arranged for

Kennedy to take the credit for the release of the Reverend Martin Luther King from a Georgia prison. But on January 5, 1961, Governor Vandiver announced that Georgia's problems were too severe for him to leave office. He withdrew his name from consideration for the federal position.[26]

There was a continuing debate among HOPE leaders over the outcome and resultant prominence of the Sibley Commission. Some recognized HOPE's support of the committee's report might taint public opinion of the panel. Fran Breeden wrote to John Sibley after one of his speeches promoting the commission's majority opinion: "I'm afraid the newspaper stories today have put us in the same pew, regardless of your desire to stand alone. I, for one, am proud that our statements were so similar in content. However, if you feel that the paper's implication that you are hand-in-glove with HOPE has damaged your considerable effectiveness, then I am truly sorry."[27]

Other members of HOPE were astonished at the usurpation of the open-school ideal by the committee and John Sibley. Muriel Lokey regarded John Sibley as a man of integrity who gave his time and acted as a vehicle with no personal risk to himself. She thought his questions at the hearings were loaded, in the "Have you stopped beating your wife?" category. He simply presided at the hearings and kept order. The commission bought time and kept the state calm, but Lokey did not see any new ideas coming out of the proceedings or their aftermath.[28]

Chapter 12

Athens to the Rescue

Either destiny or a merciful God has interposed to the state with an enormous piece of good luck.[1]

— Ralph McGill

To prepare for the opening of the legislative session in January of 1961, HOPE encouraged PTA organizations to hold question-and-answer meetings with local legislators, in order to discover the mindset of their representatives but also to inform them of their support for open schools. Half-way through such a meeting in Clayton County, four men got up from their seats and left the room. Others followed. There were as many Klansmen as PTA members in attendance at this meeting, but the local HOPE chapter did not despair. A year earlier, there would have been far fewer residents willing to even attend a HOPE-sponsored event.

Reverend James Welden, pastor of the Oak Road Methodist Church in Decatur, Georgia, signed character references for the two black students, who had applied to attend the University of Georgia, Charlayne Hunter and Hamilton Holmes. Somehow the Klan found out about Reverend Welden's letters and burned a cross on his lawn. Welden, his wife and children lay on the floor in their living room while the group of men in white robes stood outside their home.

Welden's wife asked him, "Why don't you call the police?"

Welden replied, "They're all out there on the front lawn."[2]

On January 6, 1961, the Friday prior to the opening session of the General Assembly, William A. Bootle, a federal judge in Macon, ordered the University of Georgia to enroll Hunter and Holmes immediately. Donald Hollowell and Constance Motley, lawyers working with the NAACP, had spent months in court to reach this point. After Bootle issued his order, the prospective students drove from Macon to the Athens campus with their attorneys. They entered the registrar's office, a copy of the court order in hand, and filed applications. Then they drove home to Atlanta for the weekend before returning to campus to register on Monday, January the 9th.[3]

On the morning of the 9th, campus police walked shoulder to shoulder to protect Hunter and Holmes as they made their way through throngs of unfriendly students to register. Over the weekend Governor Vandiver had dispatched Attorney General Eugene Cook to Macon to request a stay in Judge Bootle's order, and Hunter and Holmes had no sooner arrived at the registrar's office than they were informed that Judge Bootle had granted the state's petition to stop the registration process. As the two students walked to and from the registrar's office in Academic Hall, students swarmed around them, some just curious and others agitated, their chant borrowed from the women screaming at six-year-olds who entered an integrated grammar school in New Orleans: "Two-four-six-eight, We-don't-want-to-integrate."[4]

Hunter and Holmes were sent back to their homes in Atlanta as soon as the Bootle order came through, but by nightfall the scene on campus took an ugly turn. The demonstrators were now an angry mob of five hundred students and outside agitators. Some lined the track field to cheer cross burnings as others gathered at the campus arch where an effigy of Holmes was hung.

As soon as Hollowell and Motley were informed of Judge Bootle's decision to halt the registration of Holmes and Hunter, they phoned Judge Elbert Tuttle in Atlanta, the senior judge of the Fifth Circuit Court of Appeals, to ask him to overturn Judge Bootle's order and allow the registration process to continue. At 2:30 that afternoon Tuttle granted the Hollowell request, claiming Judge Bootle had no justification in preventing the registration other than the state's request.[5]

The Fifth Circuit Count of Appeals covered six Southern states, and it was a stroke of good fortune for the supporters of desegregation that the period following *Brown* included the tenure of some outstanding jurists. Judge Tuttle grew up in Hawaii, graduated from Cornell Law School, and then settled in Atlanta. He never acquired a southern accent nor did he have any prejudice against people of color. A very religious and conservative man, he neither smoked nor drank spirits and even after he became chief justice, he continued to eat lunch every day with his clerks at a table in his library — of yogurt and cheese-flavored crackers with peanut butter. Just as others for open schools had been subjected to harassment, the judge and his wife, Sara, received obscene telephone calls during this period. No matter how awful the language, Sara Tuttle always responded in her gracious southern manner: "Thank you so much for calling. We do appreciate it."[6]

Eugene Cook flew to Washington, D.C., the night of Judge Tuttle's ruling to ask Supreme Court Justice Hugo Black, who was responsible for the Fifth Circuit Court of Appeals, to overturn Judge Tuttle's decision. Justice Black denied the request on Tuesday morning, January the 9th, and Hunter and Holmes returned to the university on Tuesday afternoon to complete their registration.

The wheels were then in motion to admit black students to public universities in Georgia. However, the mandatory closing laws would require that the university be shut down as soon as Hunter and Holmes entered a classroom, and in fact, by Georgia law every public school in the state would also close. HOPE leaders knew the last chance to prevent this developing catastrophe from occurring resided with the 1961 General Assembly. It had been HOPE's position from the beginning that the massive resistance laws had to be voted down by legislators. To that end, Beverly Downing and Frances Pauley sent telegrams to every HOPE chapter in the state on Monday, January 9, with these words: "Representative Frank Twitty and Senator Carl Sanders have publicly asked to hear from the people of Georgia now on the public school issue. Urge everyone to write or wire them immediately that schools must stay open. Now is the time for maximum effort. Signed, Operation Last Chance."[7]

The scene for the open-schools debate had shifted to Athens in the previous few days, and Downing thanked her lucky stars the Barrows had agreed to take over the Athens chapter when she moved to Atlanta. James and Phyllis Barrow had supported HOPE from its beginning. James, the Athens city attorney at the time, came from a prominent Georgia family dating back to the founding of the University of Georgia. They were highly regarded in Athens, not only for their family credentials but for their active involvement in the community and at the university. Phyllis Barrow had been teaching Georgia history to university freshmen for twenty-four years.[8]

As soon as the governor learned that the students had returned to register at the University of Georgia on Tuesday afternoon, he closed the university and suspended funding to the institution. In a speech to legislators earlier in the day, he warned that he might be forced to take these unprecedented moves, insisting he did not want to foment strife in an explosive situation.

Members of the assembly were ambivalent toward the governor's address. Pierre Howard of Dekalb County said, "I never heard one man talk about so many things that don't need immediate action and so little about things that do need immediate action. He didn't tell us what his remedy is for the school situation." James Mackay expressed his concern that the governor was unwilling to call for "uninterrupted public education."[9]

The next day, Wednesday, January 11, Judge Bootle ordered the school opened and filed an injunction against Governor Vandiver, forbidding him to cut off funds to the school until a hearing on school funding laws could be held the next day.

Hunter and Holmes went to classes on Wednesday: The *Atlanta Journal* described it as "the first time that Negroes and whites have sat down together in the same classroom in a tax-supported school" [in Georgia]. The *Albany Herald* reported the situation as "an ugly abuse of federal power" and predicted the assembly would turn to the Sibley Commission recommendations in the face of the crisis. The *Athens Banner* called for an immediate end to resistance.[10] The closure of the university, the newspaper claimed, would do irreparable damage to the culture and economy of the state.

Riots broke out on the Athens campus that Wednesday night after Georgia Tech defeated Georgia in a basketball game. About two hundred young men converged outside Charlayne Hunter's dormitory (Hamilton

Holmes lived off campus) and began chanting, "Nigger, go home." Some hurled rocks through the window, and one rioter clobbered a television reporter in the face with a brick. A witness described the crowd moving "like wheat blowing in unison." Dozens of fires were set near the dormitory and in nearby woods.[11]

The Dean of Men, Bill Tate, known on campus as "Wild Bill," descended on the crowds wearing his signature red Georgia bulldog cap, demanding to see student identification cards. He was outraged that his beloved university had become a disgraceful battleground, and he was screaming at some of the students. Tate, the ubiquitous, most well-liked figure on campus, had a talent for getting along well with students, and going to bat for them on all sorts of issues, but when he saw rudeness or the slightest disorderly conduct, he showed no mercy. Therefore, it was no surprise that he took charge before the Athens police arrived at the scene, but the mayhem continued even after police intervention, some in the crowd battling the officers as they tried to control the rioting. One disturbance calmed down when police tossed a tear gas bomb into the crowd, but the melee was not over. The demonstrators began throwing rocks at people standing in front of the dormitory, and cars pulled up and the occupants threw copies of the Ku Klux Klan newspaper, *The Rebel*, into the crowd before the cars roared off again.

As soon as word circulated about the riots on the university campus, parents who feared for their children's safety began calling the dormitories, some telling their children they were coming for them or insisting they take the next bus home. Those whose children were housed in the same dormitory as Charlayne Hunter were even more upset, and some parents declared they did not want their children living with a Negro. Dean Tate's niece, who occupied a room in the same dormitory as Hunter, called her mother that night and said, "Uncle Bill's in charge. I'm just fine."[12] There were in fact a few students who welcomed Charlayne Hunter to the dormitory as the crowds outside yelled and threw rocks.

Beverly Downing received a telephone call around 11:00 P.M. from Athens that alerted her to the disaster happening right then on the university campus. At the time she was called, the riot was completely out of control, and there were few police at the scene. She phoned Betty Vinson, president of the Georgia League of Women Voters, and the two, in phone consultation with others, wrote a "Statement of Concern" over the breakdown of law and order in Athens. They then drove to the governor's executive mansion in Atlanta and rang the doorbell. Mrs. Vandiver answered the door as the governor sat in the living room reading a news-paper. Downing and Vinson explained why they were there and handed him the "Statement of Concern." It was apparent the governor had not yet heard the news of the riot. He was visibly annoyed at the women for barging in on him, and when Vinson asked him what was he going to do to maintain order, he answered, "My telephone number is in the book. Nobody called me." The women looked at him in amazement. "You aren't calling out the state patrol?" asked Vinson.

The governor replied, "Betty, you're living in an idealistic world. We are going to have violence over desegregation."

To which Vinson responded, "Yes, we're going to have violence unless you make it clear it won't be allowed." Governor Vandiver, utterly exas-perated, demanded to know if they were telling him how to run the state of Georgia.[13] After that uncomfortable moment, the women thanked the governor and left, shocked at what they had just witnessed.

The governor finally called out several units of the state patrol to quell the riot, but by the time they arrived on the scene, local police had the situation under control. Most of the rioters were led by Eldon Edwards of the U.S. Klans. He and seven other Klan members were arrested — all were armed. Thirteen students were arrested and others suspended, includ-ing Holmes and Hunter, whom Governor Vandiver explained had to leave in order to maintain the peace. They were whisked away by Dean Tate and university police, and driven back to their homes in Atlanta. The more cynical observers believed the governor wanted to allow the extreme segregationists to make their point, which he denied.[14]

Roy Harris praised the rioters. "They had the courage and the nerve to stand up in the face of federal court decrees and to defy the police and the army of Deans and get the Negroes out of the university." In another statement, Harris claimed the students, finding they could not rely on the university administration, the legislature or the governor, had simply been forced to deal with the situation on their own terms.[15] The governor responded to Harris by saying, "Rapidly growing numbers of citizens — do not want to engage in trading statements with Mr. Roy Harris."[16]

On Thursday, the night after the riots, university professors held a meeting to protest the suspension of Holmes and Hunter, and they drew up a resolution demanding the students' reinstatement. Four hundred faculty members signed the statement, and Governor Vandiver was getting pressure from other groups as well, including HOPE, to reinstate the students and end massive resistance.

Later that Thursday, during the hearing on suspension of funds to the university, Judge Bootle ruled Georgia's 1956 provision that denied state money to an integrated school unconstitutional. In response to Governor Vandiver's suspension of the students, Donald Hollowell asked Judge Bootle to reinstate Holmes and Hunter. Freeman Leverett, the state attorney, asked for time to prepare a defense of the suspension, and Judge Bootle advised Hollowell and Motley to make a written request for reinstatement and then he would issue a ruling. On Friday, Judge Bootle responded to the written request and ordered the students reinstated on Monday, January the 16th.[17]

There was a feeling of impending doom hovering over the capital and the executive mansion. The time of decision had arrived for Governor Vandiver. He had the same two choices he'd had since the school crisis began: he could defy the federal court order or comply and accept integration. On Monday, January 16, the day that Holmes and Hunter returned to the university, Governor Vandiver called legislative leaders, department heads, and other staff to convene at the executive mansion. During the deliberation, only Carl Sanders and Frank Twitty recommended that the governor abandon massive resistance and keep the university open. At the end of the meeting, the governor went around the room, shaking hands, and thanking everyone for their efforts, saying he had enjoyed working with them. The group asked the governor what was going on, and he replied that he planned to recommend the repeal of not only the mandatory school closing laws but all massive resistance legislation. He said that he knew doing so meant he would be compelled to resign. The governor also announced he would call a special session of the assembly Wednesday night to overturn the resistance laws.[18]

After most of the men left the executive mansion, a few of Vandiver's principal advisors, including Peter Zack Greer, Render Hill, and "B" Brooks, stayed behind to help prepare the Wednesday night speech before the assembly. When the meeting ended, "B" Brooks walked out the front door of the governor's mansion, paused at the small gathering of reporters and onlookers, and in his best rendition of Neville Chamberlain, opened his umbrella and said, "Gentlemen, there will be peace in our time."[19]

The next day Governor Vandiver called for a joint session of the assembly to meet at seven o'clock on Wednesday night, January 18, the first night session in the history of the state legislature. He wanted to be sure he had the largest television and radio audience possible to hear that closing schools was too big a price to pay for maintaining the status quo.

Meanwhile, John Sibley had been working to convince legislators from rural counties to step up to the plate and stop massive resistance, and in response Charles Pannel of rural Murray County started a small movement toward striking down massive resistance. He told reporters that he would sponsor a bill to continue public education and he said that he already had twenty-eight signatures and was assured of more.[20]

Governor Vandiver stood in the well of the capital before the emergency joint session of the legislature to deliver the most important address of his career. Before television cameras and a hushed audience, he outlined the futility of resisting federal law, and explained that the effects of continued resistance on the state would spread "like a cancerous growth, it will devour progress,— consuming all in its path,— pitting friend against friend,— demoralizing all that is good,— stifling economic growth of the state and denying the youth of Georgia their proper educational opportunity." He said that the federal government and courts had transformed Georgia laws from "instruments of defense to instruments of doom." He proposed the solution to the school crisis: adopt the recommendations of the Sibley Commission's majority report, and pass a "freedom of association" amendment to accompany three bills. "First, to suspend massive resistance laws and guarantee a grants-in-aid and pupil placement plan, the second to allow for local option and the third to turn control of schools over to their local school boards."[21] The governor made it clear that he hoped this proposal would maintain segregation.

Among friends from HOPE and the League of Women Voters, Frances Pauley listened to the governor from her seat in the gallery. Pauley did not feel elated. She was disgusted that "Little Ernie" spoke from both sides of his mouth, and when her friends said they must send the governor a telegram of congratulations, at first Pauley said she would not be a party to such an overture. But when one companion said, "If he's got to eat crow, he might as well have a little molasses on it," Pauley relented and sent Vandiver a telegram to congratulate him on doing the right thing.[22]

Jesse Hill, vice-president of the Atlanta Insurance Company, spoke with a reporter after the speech: "The governor might have closed Georgia State or the Atlanta high schools if they had come first, but the University of Georgia with all those legislators' sons over there and the way everybody in the state feels about it was different. He wouldn't dare close it."[23]

But the Athens campus was still in an uproar. On January 19, the Athens Ministerial Association called an emergency session to issue a formal statement against those in the legislature who recommended censure of the University of Georgia president and administration for their actions during the crisis and against a proposal to dismiss the faculty members who had supported the administration. James and Phyllis Barrow were appalled at what was happening to their beloved university and were grateful for the ministers' action, and to further the objectives of the page-long petition, they sent a letter to the parents of every university student: "HOPE's interest in the [ministers'] statement stems from its stated goal: the uninterrupted operation of the schools of Georgia in an atmosphere of calm and moderation. Parents in the state can be instrumental in achieving this goal." They asked: "Will you join with the ministers and other parents in support of the university administration?"

They suggested parents wire or write the chairman of the board of regents and the House rules committee chairman at the state capital. There were 7,000 registered undergraduate students at the University of Georgia in 1961, and a huge volume of letters and telegrams responded to the Barrow letter on both sides of the question. The Barrows heard from parents who were vitriolic in their outrage at desegregating the university as well as from those parents who backed the administration.[24]

Roy Harris tried to convince the assembly not to accept the governor's proposals. Harris accused the governor of "throwing in the towel," but the tide had turned against Harris and the segregationists. In the January 30th edition of the *Augusta Courier* the headline read: "Byrd, Sanders, Smith, Twitty, also join in irrevocable plot to race mix schools." Harris lambasted the Sibley Commission, which Vandiver had promised him was created to stall for time, and described Vandiver's speech as "an absolute proof that behind the Sibley Commission was a deliberate scheme to lay the foundation to surrender Georgia to the race mixers in 1961." The bills repealing all massive resistance laws sped through the assembly with little objection. The governor signed the bills into law on January 31, 1961.

Eleven days in January of 1961 changed the course of history in Georgia. The state tried every means they could find to block Charlayne Hunter and Hamilton Holmes from entering the University of Georgia. In the end, however, America's system of justice prevailed. Judge Bootle's rulings had followed what James Mackay had predicted the previous spring. The judge had ordered the university's funding restored and decreed Georgia's mandatory school closing laws unconstitutional, and ultimately, two college students ended segregation in Georgia's public schools.

Chapter 13

Getting Ready

We have great coping skills.[1]

— Madelyn Nix

Arch-segregationists did not give up without calls for continued resistance, and any hint of mayhem in his beloved city threw Mayor Hartsfield into near panic. He told reporters every chance he had, "Atlanta's too busy to hate. This isn't Little Rock." But the mayor knew the Klan and their followers were incensed about desegregation of Atlanta's high schools, and that no one could predict what they might do when schools opened in the fall.

The mayor's public voice of determined optimism served to keep the city calm, but he was no fool. He knew there were potentially forces beyond his control that could strike and that Atlanta could burn again. To avoid any type of violence when schools opened, HOPE, in consultation with the mayor and the League of Women Voters, NAACP and other groups, formed Organizations Assisting Schools, OASIS, in September to help city government and school officials make the transition go smoothly. Betty Vinson became the chairman of OASIS, and other HOPE leaders, especially Judy Neiman, were active in the effort. Hundreds of neighborhood coffee klatches were organized across the city to discuss potential problems and ways to avoid violence when school opened in the fall.[2] It seemed as though everyone in the city was climbing on board the desegregation bandwagon. Ministers told their congregations that desegregation gave them the opportunity to apply Christian precepts in their daily lives. Ralph McGill offered free advertising space to OASIS in the *Constitution,* and his editorials appealed to Atlantans' civic pride to help in the desegregation efforts.

HOPE sent appeals for money across the state to fund the remaining work to be done. One such mailing caused a furor among GUTS supporters. Marvin Griffin, a former governor and old-time Georgia politician, headed a column in the *Bainbridge Post-Searchlight*: "Loose Talk Is Dangerous." He condemned the "Atlanta-sponsored HOPE organization" for sending solicitations throughout Georgia for money to be used against riots: "This is dangerous talk and HOPE enthusiasts should be severely reprimanded for irresponsible action — this should not be tolerated." Griffin said that opponents of desegregation should be allowed to demonstrate against the orders of the court just as much as the NAACP had been doing. The HOPE mailing to which Griffin referred included a photo of a police confrontation with rioting crowds in New Orleans with the caption: "Police at New Orleans Quell 2,000, Jailing 58. Don't Let It Happen Here!"[3]

* * *

A bad case of the flu kept Madelyn Nix out of Booker T. Washington High School the day representatives from the NAACP made the announcement to the student body about the procedures for applying as transfer students for the following year. Upon returning to school, Nix found out that black students were finally able to apply for a transfer to the better white high schools after Judge Hooper ordered Atlanta to desegregate in the fall. One had to be living in a cave not to know about the court case to desegregate Atlanta's high schools that had been taking place for several years and the subsequent battles of resistance in the state legislature, but this was the news that many black teenagers had been waiting to hear.

Madelyn Nix was encouraged to apply to one of Atlanta's white high schools by her teachers and other adults close to her. She came from a middle-class family who lived on the Morehouse College campus. She was not only an excellent student but also likable, easygoing and ambitious. Nix completed the application in early May to transfer as a twelfth grader. May 15, 1961 was the deadline for turning in the forms.

The Atlanta Board of Education had given itself the month of May to complete the process of determining which black applicants would be selected as transfer students to the 11th and 12th grades in four white high schools. The educators planned for the process to move along quickly and to be completed by the start of summer vacation. The idea was to give the selected transfer students enough time to absorb what might be in store for them the following fall and to prepare accordingly.

Those who lived in southern cities, including Atlanta, had learned from the violent upheaval in New Orleans the previous fall as first-graders desegregated four white schools. Inadequate preparation and dubious strategies in New Orleans had paved the way for lamentable results. Parents removed their children from the William Frantz school as soon as one black child, Ruby Bridges, entered the first grade, leaving her alone in the classroom to be taught by a white teacher the entire year.[4] This served as a parable of sorts for Atlantans, and the OASIS organization worked to help both whites and blacks in Atlanta achieve a better result than their neighboring city.

Of the 300 transfer forms taken by black students, 132 students actually applied for transfer. After turning in her application, Madelyn Nix learned that all transfer applicants were required to take a series of academic tests the following Thursday. The tests were to last four hours with an additional three hours of tests on Friday. Nix went into the test phase of the process with a relaxed attitude, not concentrating on the outcome.

A week later Madelyn Nix received a letter from the board of education congratulating her on having passed the first phase of the selection process. She was required to take another test to determine her ability to learn and to participate in psychological testing, which would show how she handled stress and would gauge her emotional makeup.

The notion of actually attending an all-white high school was beginning to sink in with Nix. She and her parents assumed she would attend college, and everyone in the black community knew their high schools were inferior to white schools and could not prepare students as well. To spend her last year in a better equipped and tougher academic setting appealed to Madelyn, but it was not something she had ever given much thought to until she found herself in the latter stages of the selection process to be one of the first black students to attend school with whites.

Following the second phase of testing, another letter of congratulations came to Madelyn Nix, stating that she had done well in this stage of the process as well. No names of students had been released to the media, for everyone involved in the selection process was well aware of the potential threats and actual danger that might be directed to these black families by the die-hard segregationists on the lunatic fringe.

There was still another hurdle for Madelyn and the other applicants to clear before the final selection was made. Each candidate would be interviewed.

A representative from the board of education, a psychologist, and a lawyer were seated behind a table addressing Nix, who was directly across from them. Part way through the interview the psychologist posed the following question to the young student:

"You know, Madelyn, you'll be one of very few Negro students going to Brown High and we cannot guarantee your safety. How will you conduct yourself, say, if girls are waiting for you in the restroom?"

"They'll probably say hello and that's all," she answered without hesitation. Nix was looking on the bright side, but she wondered how the boys would answer the same question.

Nix noticed the psychologist writing on a pad every time she put her hands in her lap and when she placed them on top of the table as if those movements were significant. A week later Madelyn Nix received a letter announcing she had been accepted as one of the students to transfer to Brown High School the following fall.[5]

Another Booker T. Washington student, Tom Welch, with the encouragement of his parents, filled out the form to transfer as an 11th grader. The Welches lived in a solid working-class neighborhood. His father owned a service station two doors down from Pascals, a popular soul food restaurant where leaders in the black community gathered daily to consume their favorite specialties of fried chicken, greens, and macaroni and cheese and to talk about the issues of the day. Many of Pascal's customers patronized the service station too, where Welch's father joined in the conversations that focused on the topic of the times—desegregating Atlanta schools. Welch, although successful in terms of the black community, wanted more for his son and to move up and out required better education than segregated schools offered.

Tom Welch had heard that white high schools ran ROTC programs, and there were none at black schools. Welch was the rare kind of youngster who was actually planning his future in high school. ROTC classes might provide an edge when applying to colleges as well as good preparation for the military in case he went into the armed services.

As was the case for Madelyn Nix, Tom Welch was a good student. He passed the round of academic and psychological tests with ease. During the interview session, he was asked: "How do you think you will react to students who may be hostile to you?" Welch had never had a reason to get into fights. He was aware that Atlanta's leaders in the black and white community were fixated on handling desegregation smoothly, especially without any violence. The Little Rock and New Orleans fiascoes were never far from their minds.

"I figure there'll be some who won't like my being at their school and might try to push me around, but I'm not going to do anything back at them," Welch replied.[6]

The selection committee wanted to make sure that the students, the boys in particular, who were transferring to white schools were not troublemakers, but rather, that these young people would keep their frustration to themselves, and endure taunting without striking back. The questioners knew, however, that even if a young man or woman gave the "correct" answers, there were no guarantees that these black students would actually act as they said they would when in the line of fire.

Tom Welch received a letter of congratulations on being one of the students selected to transfer to white schools in the fall. It was a proud day for the Welch family.[7]

Of the 132 students who submitted transfer applications, only ten students were selected, three boys and seven girls. The students represented the three black high schools in Atlanta: Donita Gaines, Domaris Allen and Arthur Simmons from Turner High School; Lawrence Jefferson and Martha Holmes, Mary McMullen and Rosalyn Walton from Howard

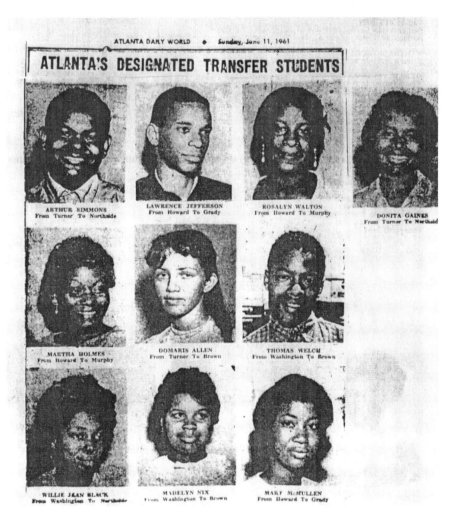

ATLANTA DAILY WORLD • Sunday, June 11, 1961

ATLANTA'S DESIGNATED TRANSFER STUDENTS

ARTHUR SIMMONS
From Turner To Northside

LAWRENCE JEFFERSON
From Howard To Grady

ROSALYN WALTON
From Howard To Murphy

DONITA GAINES
From Turner To Northside

MARTHA HOLMES
From Howard To Murphy

DOMARIS ALLEN
From Turner To Brown

THOMAS WELCH
From Washington To Brown

WILLIE JEAN BLACK
From Washington To Northside

MADELYN NIX
From Washington To Brown

MARY McMULLEN
From Howard To Grady

Atlanta's designated transfer students. June 11, 1961. Courtesy of the *Atlanta Daily World*.

High School; and Willie Jean Black, Tom Welch and Madelyn Nix from Washington High School. They would be transferring to one of four white schools: Murphy High School, Northside High School, Brown High School, or Grady High School.

The ten transfer students were typical teenagers who loved music, sports, and their social lives, but they were not typical in their decision to be pioneers in removing the stigma of segregation from their community. These young people were not fully aware of what they were getting into until the reality of it all became utterly clear during the summer of 1961. (One of the ten students selected, Domaris Allen, dropped out of the program).

HOPE took an active role in preparing students for the transition in the fall. With the help of the director of Quaker House, John Youngblut, Betty Harris and other volunteers organized get-acquainted events at the meeting house for the black transfer students, and they selected white students from high schools that were to be integrated in the fall to attend as well. The idea was to provide a friendly arena in which the students could get to know one another as teenagers, a place to discuss the positive and negative aspects of going to an integrated school and to share common interests over a coke and cookies.[8] Quaker House was one of two locations in the city at that time where interracial meetings were tolerated, and it must be remembered that for white and black students to gather in the same room for any reason was a radical concept in 1961.

Betty Harris led in this effort at Quaker House due to her experience in organizing adult interracial events in her church and with Girl Scout volunteers (although less successfully in this latter case). Harris invited her friend, the well-known Georgia author, Lillian Smith, to speak to the teenagers. Smith, a vibrant public speaker, aroused her student audience into thinking and discussing ways to better relations between the races, which she said only they were able to achieve. The local NAACP president spoke to the group, a local theater troupe performed socio-dramas involving racial encounters, and Dr. Benjamin Mays, president of Morehouse College, gave an inspirational talk.[9]

The Quaker meetings were important to transfer students because of the interaction they had with friendly white students. The speakers and programs provided the vehicle for tearing down suppositions they may have had about what to expect from most whites.

The families of the transfer students received abusive phone calls after students' names were announced to the public. Tom Welch's mother became upset when callers used obscenities while threatening "I'm gonna kill your son." Atlanta's police force, concerned about the potential danger, patrolled the neighborhoods of these students night and day. Madelyn Nix became accustomed to seeing a formation of official cars around the Morehouse College campus. The lead car was a marked police car, the second was unmarked, the third was another marked police car and the fourth was a paddy wagon.

The black students were busy that summer. The board of education held mandatory sessions wherein the students were drilled on how to behave the first day of school, how to dress, and how to handle aggressive acts. They role-played situations in which the transfers were taunted by white students. The psychologist discussed with them what they feared most about entering the white environment, and offered suggestions for how to cope with the fear and the isolation they would probably experience.

In short, these teenagers were expected to be model students. Much was riding on their performance, and expectations ran high from members of their own community — from Atlanta's leaders who wanted to show the world that their city was not Little Rock or New Orleans, and from the many HOPE volunteers who had worked to keep schools open in Georgia — all of them wanted to prove that this first step in desegregation could take place without violence. Although during the previous winter Charlayne Hunter and Hamilton Holmes had broken the color barrier as college students at the University of Georgia, an even bigger change in public education was about to take place, potentially involving all school-age children in the state. The transfer students would join Hunter and Holmes as pioneers in fulfilling the rights of black citizens to be educated in a desegregated setting.

Chapter 14

A New Day in Georgia

Everything is normal—No one is eating with them.[1]
— High school principals

The time had finally arrived. It was Wednesday, August 30, 1961, the day that marked the culmination of black leaders' persistent fight for educational equality and Georgia's final acceptance of federal law. Nine black teenagers were entering four white high schools in Atlanta, and much was riding on the success of the first day. Members of the press from around the country were poised to report on how the city of Atlanta had adapted to the modern world. A hundred years before, the city had risen from ashes to become a commercial and cosmopolitan dynamo. Would it now show the world it was ready to behave in a civil way as it moved from separate and anything-but-equal to a desegregated system that could provide a fair education for all its citizens?

The day before, Police Chief Jenkins had staged a full-scale rehearsal of security measures to be used the first day of school. The early morning trial-run sent officers on motorcycles to their posts at every high school to be desegregated, and there they tested communication channels and went over the rituals of escorting the transfer students into the buildings. Chief Jenkins told the press he had never seen such complete cooperation and tight organization in this city.[2]

Outside Madelyn Nix's home on the Morehouse College campus, a police car waited to escort her to Brown High. The Nix family had grown accustomed to seeing Atlanta police cars drive by their house several times a day. Police Chief Jenkins had ordered a four-vehicle police patrol to cover the campus day and night. The homes of other transfer students were similarly patrolled. The city had learned how crucial an organized show of force would be in thwarting civil disturbance from the out-of-control mob disasters of Little Rock and New Orleans.

Madelyn Nix kissed her parents good-bye as they stood in the front yard.[3] She walked to the open car door and turned around to wave to her parents, photographers, and other onlookers, then slid into the back seat and stared straight ahead. She had left her support behind and now she was on her own. It was not a long ride to Brown High, but time enough for random thoughts to run through her mind. She remembered her mother's alarmed face when city police came to the door to warn her not to go into the community because pictures of transfer students had been published in the paper and they could not guarantee her safety. Her mother's expression turned from alarm to fright when the officer asked her which state she would prefer to send her daughter to in case of an emergency.[4] In the back of the police car, the teenager smiled. She felt excitement and some anxiety, but she was not afraid.

The officer stopped the car in front of Brown High. Madelyn did not expect to see students standing outside. Transfer students were scheduled to arrive a few minutes after the bell rang, so the halls would be cleared. Madelyn walked into the building without incident. At the end of the school day a few minutes before the closing bell, Madelyn and the other two transfer pupils left the school premises and were driven home in unmarked police cars.

That Wednesday morning across town in the affluent Buckhead section, Fran Breeden, Muriel Lokey, Betty Harris, and other HOPE leaders gathered at a member's home situated a block from Northside High. It was possible to see the school from the living room picture windows. The press was required to stay a precise distance from school buildings, and WSB television stationed itself on this "HOPE property" to take long distance-shots of the three transfer students walking toward the school entrance. As soon as the students arrived safely inside, the HOPE crowd cheered and raised their coffee cups in celebration.

A city hall employee looked into the aldermen's chamber and exclaimed, "They must be expecting more Yankees than Sherman brought in."[5] It was part of Mayor Hartsfield's no-nonsense policy to set up press headquarters at City Hall, where teletypes, typewriters, radios connected to police cars, and telephones were made available to the local and out-of-town press corps to keep them away from the schools. The mayor became the genial host of a big party, offering Smithfield ham and hot biscuits, coffee, and, of course, Atlanta's beverage, Coke, along with other soft drinks and fruit juices. At the end of the day, sightseeing buses were provided for those who wished to see more of the city, and the mayor

Atlanta City Hall press conference: City officials announcing to the national media the peaceful desegregation of four high schools. August 30, 1961. Mayor William Hartsfield standing beneath the seal, Superintendent John Letson speaking on the phone and Police Chief Herbert Jenkins (white arrow). Courtesy of the Lane Brothers Photographers Collection, Special Collections and Archives, Georgia State University Library.

extended an invitation to a cocktail party at the Biltmore Hotel, which he explained to the out-of-towners as "what we in Georgia call a buttermilk party." Throughout the day Hartsfield lived up to his colorful reputation, speaking in the salty Georgia vernacular, reveling in his role as ringmaster of Atlanta's biggest show. He called the troublemakers "the outhouse gang" and the "two-hole toilet crowd," pegging them as "visitors" from rural areas.[6] He claimed it was his idea in the name of hospitality to provide everything the press could possibly need in one big room at City Hall. This way he could control events, rather than having to react to them.

Dr. John Letson was elected superintendent of Atlanta city schools in June of 1960 following the retirement of Dr. Ira Jarrell who had held the position since 1944. Letson and his deputy took turns presiding over the day-long event at city hall. They were in communication with the four high school principals when the transfer students arrived, after lunch, and when school ended. The telephone conversations were broadcast over a loudspeaker, after which Letson invited the reporters to ask any questions of the principals they might have.

Charlayne Hunter, a journalism major at the University of Georgia, was covering the day's events for the Atlanta black newspaper, *Atlanta Inquirer*. She spoke with a reporter about the show of violence during her first days at the university the previous winter. She said she was "not sorry it went that way now that it's over." Hunter added that knowing desegregation could erupt into fights contributed to Atlanta's long-range preparation for a peaceful transition.

Hunter looked for Betty Vinson in the press room, having heard about her trip to see the governor the night of the riots on the university campus. They met, exchanged stories, and remained together throughout the day. Later that morning, the two women laughed as they peacefully desegregated the restrooms in City Hall. There were no restrooms labeled "colored" in sight.

Hunter spoke about the nine transfer students with whom she had become well acquainted during the summer, visiting them in their homes at night and often having lunch with them. She told Vinson that her contacts with the students were in a light vein. "What could I really tell them?"

But she said, "When they walked up the walks to those schools this morning my heart was with them."[7]

The transition to the integration of four Atlanta high schools happened quietly for the most part. It was reported that some courtesy was demonstrated at Brown High when a few white students got up and introduced themselves to the black transfer students in the lunch room.[8] Four teenagers were arrested near Murphy High School after they failed to obey a police order to clear the premises. Police found a pistol and a claw hammer in one of the youth's cars. Another young man, who claimed he was a Nazi storm trooper and wanted to give out Nazi literature, was arrested near Grady High after he refused to leave the scene. The five men were taken to municipal court and charged with interfering with Atlanta's school desegregation. Later in the afternoon Police Chief Jenkins allowed the press to witness the line-up of the arrested youths, and Vinson and Hunter joined other reporters at the municipal court building. Betty Vinson felt her stomach tighten as she watched the Nazi click his heels and shout, "Heil Hitler."[9] All five men were convicted and received sentences from 30 to 60 days in the city jail.

An angry father arrived outside Grady High in the afternoon, carrying a yard-long switch. He told the police he planned to use it on his thirteen-year-old daughter who disobeyed him and had gone to the integrated school. The father was prevented from entering the school and told to go home. The Grady High principal was informed that the father threatened "to cut the blood from her with a switch" when his daughter returned home from school. The father told the police officers he didn't have anything against Negroes, "but I do against the federal government."[10]

In mid-afternoon Mayor Hartsfield grabbed the microphone in the press headquarters and announced to the phalanx of reporters: "We told you we'd give you the news. Listen. Stop the press. The City Hall is being picketed." The mayor then chuckled as he watched reporters go outside to see the commotion. On the sidewalk in front of the building were three men carrying signs: "Fight Jewish Communism and Race Mixing," "Parents and Pupils Boycott Mixed Schools" and "Wake Up, White America."[11] The small showing did not make the evening news.

As the schools closed for the day, President Kennedy began a press conference in Washington by saluting Georgia citizens, Atlantans in particular, and officials for their "courage, tolerance, and above all, respect for the law."[12] He paid tribute to Governor Vandiver, Mayor Hartsfield, Police Chief Jenkins, and Dr. Letson, the superintendent of schools.

Throughout this historic day, the loudspeaker in the press room bellowed the words of high school principals: "Everything is normal." "No one is eating with them." "No one is speaking to them." "I repeat — everything is normal." Through intermittent static, the same words came through. Betty Vinson, although grateful for the peaceful transition, was dismayed to think that isolating the black students was viewed as the "normal" way to behave.

Nevertheless, HOPE volunteers were exhilarated and grateful for the peaceful changeover, but it had been a long battle, and they were exhausted. Muriel Lokey remarked that she felt everybody who had worked for so long in HOPE had been tossed like waves on a beach — some days there were ups and other days there were downs. The members of HOPE welcomed a rest from the telephone, from working the capital building, from making speeches, from organizing and going to meetings, forums, and conferences, from writing letters, press releases, brochures, and from worrying about how they would pay for it all. Fran Breeden and other HOPE leaders thanked Betty Harris for steering them in the right direction and keeping them on track, for her ability to see the big picture while managing the innumerable details of running a statewide organization and for doing it all with a gracious intelligence.

But before they disbanded HOPE and settled back to ordinary life, they decided to kick up their heels and celebrate. It seemed fitting to invite all their supporters for cocktails and dinner at the Dinkler-Plaza Hotel in Atlanta. Nan Pendergrast wrote the invitation:[13]

> The air is full of fall out:
> the woods are full of spies.
> The courts are full of lawsuits,
> the Russians full of lies.
> Berlin is full of tension,
> And Africa's aflame.
> But Georgia, bless her heart, has made herself a name.
> She's run HOPE out of business,

in the best way we could ask.
Now each of us is free to choose another noble task.
But before we launch ourselves
into the next consuming cause,
We need a brief hiatus — a nice refreshing pause.

Epilogue

Forty years after the struggle to keep public schools open and deseg-regated, a reporter asked Maxine Friedman what would have happened if there had been no HOPE. She answered without hesitation, "The schools would have closed."[1] There were ample reasons for HOPE volunteers to pat themselves on the back, but one volunteer expressed what many felt: "We did it because we had to. We filled a void."

A few regrets mingled among the well-deserved congratulations, how-ever. Fran Breeden spoke with the Reverend Martin Luther King at his Nobel Peace Prize celebration in Atlanta, saying she was sorry HOPE could not include black volunteers in their fight to keep the schools open. King responded, "You had no choice. I want to thank you and HOPE for what you did."[2] The former HOPE leader breathed a sigh of gratitude and relief. But there were other misgivings, too. Muriel Lokey said the HOPE women she worked with were energized and fueled by the belief that legal segre-gation was wrong, and yet they could not say so, but instead had to cen-ter their fight on keeping the schools open. Years after HOPE was disbanded, Nan Pendergrast lamented that if they had known back in 1961 that desegregation of the Atlanta schools would turn out as it did, "it would have broken our hearts."[3] From 1961 onward, Atlanta desegregated their schools, but at a snail's pace, one grade at a time. Meanwhile, white families were fleeing the city to the white suburbs, which left city schools with mostly black students.

Governor Ernest Vandiver never held public office again, just as he had predicted when he called for repeal of the resistance laws before the 1961 General Assembly. However, in addition to fighting school desegre-gation and then presiding over it, he is credited for having cleaned up the corruption left over from his predecessor, Marvin Griffin's term in office. Vandiver entered the governor's race in 1966 but withdrew for health reasons. He also ran for the United States Senate in 1972 but finished third. Governor Vandiver remarked after he left office that HOPE had been right all along.[4] He died February 21, 2005 at age 86.

On February 5, 1965, Judge Frank A. Hooper ordered Lester Maddox, one of HOPE's most vociferous critics, to either serve blacks at his Atlanta restaurant, 'Pickwick Cafeteria,' or he would have it closed. Maddox refused the order and closed the restaurant himself.[5] He became governor of Georgia in 1967.

HOPE women had been brought up with the American volunteer ethic, so it was not surprising that they continued to serve Atlanta in many ways. Beverly Downing Long became active in the mental health field, applying many of the techniques and strategies she had learned in HOPE, asking questions such as: "How do you make things happen? How do you change minds?" Muriel Lokey and Frances Pauley worked with Atlanta's poor and disadvantaged, the majority of whom were blacks. Betty Harris became program director in the Atlanta branch of the YWCA, where she organized interracial events for children and adults. Nan Pendergrast became active at Quaker House and in the peace movement. Fran Breeden continued her work with the Junior League and the Greater Atlanta Council of Churches. She was honored for her leadership role in HOPE by being named Woman of the Year in 1961.

Being active in the community has always played a large role in the lives of HOPE women. They would agree with Donald Hollowell, who said upon receiving an award for his lifetime service as a civil rights lawyer, "I'm just glad I was able to render a little service, because that's what we're here on earth for." [6]

Madelyn Nix spent one lonely year at Brown High. An FBI agent accompanied her to and from school and stayed near her at all times. Once, she recalled, a student splashed a Coke on her, and another time a lab mouse was stuck in her face as she walked down the hall, but she called these incidents merely "pranks." She said she was prepared for much worse to happen, but the isolation was hard to endure at times. Only three white students were friendly to her. She recalled that one girl remarked to her half-way through the first year, "You aren't anything like we thought you'd be." She also remembered with a chuckle that she did have options. She could have elected to participate in senior class activities, in which case everyone else would stay home or if she did not go to these events, all other seniors would participate. She did, however, participate in graduation ceremonies, knowing that the white students would not have missed that event for anything. She remembered a girl whispered to her as they were waiting to walk down the aisle together at graduation that her father would be shocked when he saw her with Madelyn, but the girl concluded, "Don't worry. We'll get through it and I'll catch it later." Madelyn Nix-Beamen is now a corporate attorney in Pennsylvania.

Tom Welch, who also went to Brown High, experienced isolation and endured a few abusive incidents. In an ROTC class, for example, a student spit on Welch and announced in a loud voice, "I spit on a nigger." Welch then heard a noisy discussion in the office of student officers and the commandant. Soon afterward, the commandant apologized to Welch for the student's behavior and said, "You will not have to worry about that cadet again."

Welch also remembered the contrast in how teachers reacted to his presence. In some classrooms the students would move as far away from him as possible without the teacher's objection, but one teacher told the class she would not tolerate such behavior — students were to take their assigned seats and get to work.[7] Tom Welch has a master's degree in city planning from Massachusetts Institute of Technology and is now a real estate developer in Boston.

Donita Gaines-Ball, a Northside High transfer student, was the only transfer student who decided to return to her home school, Turner High. She said many years later, "I felt torn, as if it was up to me to prove all blacks were equal. That creates a lot of stress for a sixteen-year-old."[8]

Martha Holmes-Jackson said to a reporter who reminded her that thirty years before she had integrated Murphy High, "[It] will just be another day, but I will think back on what we did and the progress we made to our race — I will smile, maybe a little brighter."[9] Martha Holmes-Jackson graduated from Spelman College and became a third-grade teacher in the Atlanta school system.

Rosalyn Walton-Lees attended Murphy High and became a system's manager for the Internal Revenue Service in Atlanta.

The tenth student, Damarius Allen, selected as a transfer, decided to take early admissions to Spelman College instead of entering Brown High. Later she joined the Foreign Service Bureau in cultural affairs.

The effects of this turbulent period in the nation's history can still be seen. Black children who were denied an education in Prince Edward County, Virginia, in 1959 were given scholarships in 2005 as reparation for their loss. The cost of these scholarships was financed by an individual donation of one million dollars matched by state funds. One person taking advantage of the offer was Warren Brown, age 51, who planned to attend college to study criminal justice. During the school crisis, Warren's mother kept him at home until she could find a local church who offered classes to black children.[10]

The Little Rock school district was released from federal supervision

" THIS WAY! "

"This Way." *Atlanta Constitution*, 1972. Clifford H. "Baldy" Baldowski Editorial Cartoons. Courtesy of the Richard B. Russell Library for Political Research and Studies, University of Georgia Libraries.

in 2007, nearly fifty years after President Eisenhower sent in troops to escort nine black students into all-white Central High School.[11]

Atlanta's peaceful transition to desegregation of its public schools prevented lingering racial unrest in the city that afflicted other places, such as Boston after its busing controversy. The leaders of Atlanta and groups such as HOPE made a lasting contribution to the civility of the city they loved.

When she spoke to various civic groups about the desegregation battle in the years following her HOPE involvement, Frances Pauley told the story of a black boy and a white boy waiting at a school bus stop in rural Georgia. The white boy blurts out, "I wish my skin was as black as yours." The black boy answers, "Why?" And the white boy responds, "Because then I wouldn't have to feel so bad when people are mean to you."

Appendix 1

Majority and Minority Opinions in Plessy v. Ferguson *United States Supreme Court Decision, 1896**

Introduction to the Court Opinion on the *Plessy v. Ferguson* Case[†]

There has been an ongoing debate among historians over the origins of racial segregation in this country in the decades after emancipation. One group of scholars has argued that segregation was not a predestined pattern of racial relations in the post-war South. White masters and black slaves had lived and worked in close proximity before the Civil War, and a variety of patterns of racial relations existed in the 1870s and 1880s. Although southern states did not erect the legal structures that supported an extensive system of social, economic and political segregation until the 1890s, white hostility had permeated southern race relations for over two centuries. What is certain is that the traditions of racism, white hostility toward blacks and the inability of the black minority to protect itself after northern troops went home disadvantaged the former slaves from the start.

**Majority and Minority Opinions from* Plessy v. Ferguson, *Federal Archives 163 U.S. 537 (1886)*.
[†]*http://odur.let.rug.nl/~usa/D/1876–1900/plessy/plessy_i.htm*

Every southern state had enacted black codes immediately after the war to keep the former slaves under tight control. After these had been voided by the Union, white southerners began exploring other means to maintain their supremacy over blacks. Southern legislatures enacted criminal statutes that invariably prescribed harsher penalties for blacks than for whites convicted of the same crime, and erected a system of peonage that survived into the early twentieth century.

In an 1878 case, the Supreme Court ruled that the states could not prohibit segregation on common carriers, such as railroads, streetcars or steamboats. Twelve years later, it approved a Mississippi statute requiring segregation on intrastate carriers. In doing so it acquiesced in the South's solution to race relations.

In the best known of the early segregation cases, *Plessy v. Ferguson* (1896), Justice Billings Brown asserted that distinctions based on race ran afoul of neither the Thirteenth or Fourteenth Amendments, two of the Civil War amendments passed to abolish slavery and secure the legal rights of the former slaves.

Although nowhere in the opinion can the phrase "separate but equal" be found, the Court's rulings approved legally enforced segregation as long as the law did not make facilities for blacks inferior to those of whites.

In his famous and eloquent dissent, Justice Harlan protested that states could not impose criminal penalties on a citizen simply because he or she wished to use the public highways and common carriers. Such laws defeated the whole purpose of the Civil War amendments. His pleas that the "Constitution is color-blind" fell on deaf ears.

For further reading: C. Vann Woodward, *The Strange Career of Jim Crow* (2nd ed., 1966); William Gillette, *Retreat from Reconstruction* (1979); and Charles A. Lofgren, *The Plessy Case* (1987).

Plessy v. Ferguson (1896)

Justice Brown delivered the opinion of the Court.

This case turns upon the constitutionality of an act of the General Assembly of the State of Louisiana, passed in 1890, providing for separate railway carriages for the white and colored races....

The constitutionality of this act is attacked upon the ground that it conflicts both with the Thirteenth Amendment of the Constitution, abolishing slavery, and the Fourteenth Amendment, which prohibits certain restrictive legislation on the part of the States.

1. That it does not conflict with the Thirteenth Amendment, which abolished slavery and involuntary servitude, except as a punishment for crime, is too clear for argument....

The proper construction of the 14th amendment was first called to the attention of this court in the Slaughter-house cases, ... which involved, however, not a question of race, but one of exclusive privileges. The case did not call for any expression of opinion as to the exact rights it was intended to secure to the colored race, but it was said generally that its main purpose was to establish the citizenship of the negro; to give definitions of citizenship of the United States and of the States, and to protect from the hostile legislation of the States the privileges and immunities of citizens of the United States, as distinguished from those of citizens of the States.

The object of the amendment was undoubtedly to enforce the absolute equality of the two races before the law, but in the nature of things it could not have been intended to abolish distinctions based upon color, or to enforce social, as distinguished from political equality, or a commingling of the two races upon terms unsatisfactory to either. Laws permitting, and even requiring, their separation in places where they are liable to be brought into contact do not necessarily imply the inferiority of either race to the other, and have been generally, if not universally, recognized as within the competency of the state legislatures in the exercise of their police power. The most common instance of this is connected with the establishment of separate schools for white and colored children, which has been held to be a valid exercise of the legislative power even by courts of States where the political rights of the colored race have been longest and most earnestly enforced....

So far, then, as a conflict with the Fourteenth Amendment is concerned, the case reduces itself to the question whether the statute of Louisiana is a reasonable regulation, and with respect to this there must necessarily be a large discretion on the part of the legislature. In determining the question of reasonableness it is at liberty to act with reference to the established usages, customs and traditions of the people, and with a view to the promotion of their comfort, and the preservation of the public peace and good order. Gauged by this standard, we cannot say that a law which authorizes or even requires the separation of the two races in public conveyances is unreasonable, or more obnoxious to the Fourteenth Amendment than the acts of Congress requiring separate schools for colored children in the District of Columbia, the constitutionality of which does not seem to have been questioned, or the corresponding acts of state legislatures.

We consider the underlying fallacy of the plaintiff's argument to consist in the assumption that the enforced separation of the two races stamps the colored race with a badge of inferiority. If this be so, it is not by reason of any-thing found in the act, but solely because the colored race chooses to put that construction upon it. The argument necessarily assumes that if, as has been more than once the case, and is not unlikely to be so again, the colored race should become the dominant power in the state legislature, and should enact a law in precisely similar terms, it would thereby relegate the white race to an inferior position. We imagine that the white race, at least, would not acquiesce in this assumption. The argument also assumes that social prejudices may be overcome by legislation, and that equal rights cannot be secured to the negro except by an enforced commingling of the two races. We cannot accept this proposition. If the two races are to meet upon terms of social equality, it must be the result of natural affinities, a mutual appreciation of each other's merits and a voluntary consent of individuals.... Legislation is powerless to eradicate racial instincts or to abolish distinctions based upon physical differences, and the attempt to do so can only result in accentuating the difficulties of the present situation. If the civil and political rights of both races be equal one cannot be inferior to the other civilly or politically. If one race be inferior to the other socially, the Constitution of the United States cannot put them upon the same plane....

Justice Harlan, dissenting.

While there may be in Louisiana persons of different races who are not citizens of the United States, the words in the act, "white and colored races," necessarily include all citizens of the United States of both races residing in that State. So that we have before us a state enactment that compels, under penalties, the separation of the two races in railroad passenger coaches, and makes it a crime for a citizen of either race to enter a coach that has been assigned to citizens of the other race....

In respect of civil rights, common to all citizens, the Constitution of the United States does not, I think, permit any public authority to know the race of those entitled to be protected in the enjoyment of such rights. Every true man has pride of race, and under appropriate circumstances when the rights of others, his equals before the law, are not to be affected, it is his privilege to express such pride and to take such action based upon it as to him seems proper. But I deny that any legislative body or judicial tribunal may have regard to the race of citizens when the civil rights of those citizens are not involved. Indeed, such legislation, as that here in question, is inconsistent not only with that equality of rights which pertains to citizenship, National and State, but with the personal liberty enjoyed by every one within the United States....

The white race deems itself to be the dominant race in this country. And so it is, in prestige, in achievements, in education, in wealth and in power. So, I doubt not, it will continue to be for all time, if it remains true to its great heritage and holds fast to the principles of constitutional liberty. But in view of the Constitution, in the eye of the law, there is in this country no superior, dominant, ruling class of citizens. There is no caste here. Our Constitution is color-blind, and neither knows nor tolerates classes among citizens. In respect of civil rights, all citizens are equal before the law. The humblest is the peer of the most powerful. The law regards man as man, and takes no account of his surroundings or of his color when his civil rights as guaranteed by the supreme law of the land are involved. It is, therefore, to be regretted that this high tribunal, the final expositor of the fundamental law of the land, has reached the conclusion that it is competent for a State to regulate the enjoyment by citizens of their civil rights solely upon the basis of race.

In my opinion, the judgment this day rendered will, in time, prove to be quite as pernicious as the decision made by this tribunal in the Dred Scott case.... The present decision, it may well be apprehended, will not only stimulate aggressions, more or less brutal and irritating, upon the admitted rights of colored citizens, but will encourage the belief that it is possible, by means of state enactments, to defeat the beneficent purposes which the people of the United States had in view when they adopted the recent amendments of the Constitution, by one of which the blacks of this country were made citizens of the United States and of the States in which they respectively reside, and whose privileges and immunities, as citizens, the States are forbidden to abridge. Sixty millions of whites are in no danger from the presence here of eight millions of blacks. The destinies of the two races, in this country, are indissolubly linked together, and the interests of both require that the common government of all shall not permit the seeds of race hate to be planted under the sanction of law. What can more certainly arouse race hate, what more certainly create and perpetuate a feeling of distrust between these races, than state enactments, which, in fact, proceed on the ground that colored citizens are so inferior and degraded that they cannot be allowed to sit in public coaches occupied by white citizens? That, as all will admit, is the real meaning of such legislation as was enacted in Louisiana....

If evils will result from the commingling of the two races upon public highways established for the benefit of all, they will be infinitely less than those that will surely come from state legislation regulating the enjoyment of civil rights upon the basis of race. We boast of the freedom enjoyed by our people above all other peoples. But it is difficult to reconcile that boast with a state of the law which, practically, puts the brand of servitude and degradation upon a large class of our fellow-citizens, our equals before the law....

I am of opinion that the statute of Louisiana is inconsistent with the personal liberty of citizens, white and black, in that State, and hostile to both the spirit and letter of the Constitution of the United States. If laws of like character should be enacted in the several States of the Union, the effect would be in the highest degree mischievous. Slavery, as an institution tolerated by law would, it is true, have disappeared from our country, but there would remain a power in the States, by sinister legislation, to interfere with the full enjoyment of the blessings of freedom; to regulate civil rights, common to all citizens upon the basis of race; and to place in a condition of legal inferiority a large body of American citizens, now constituting a part of the political community called the People of the United States, for whom, and by whom through representatives, our government is administered.

Appendix 2

Opinion in Brown v. Board of Education *United States Supreme Court Decision, 1954**

Introduction to the Court Opinion on the Brown v. Board of Education Case†

The National Association for the Advancement of Colored People (NAACP), the leading civil rights organization in the country, had never accepted the legitimacy of the "separate but equal" rule, and in the 1940s and 1950s had brought a series of cases designed to show that separate facilities did not meet the equality criterion. In *McLaurin v. Oklahoma State Regents* (1950), a unanimous Supreme Court had struck down University of Oklahoma rules that had permitted a black man to attend classes, but fenced him off from other students. That same day, the Court ruled in *Sweatt v. Painter* that a makeshift law school the state of Texas had created to avoid admitting blacks into the prestigious University of Texas Law School did not come anywhere close to being equal. Whatever else the justices knew about segregated facilities, they did know what made a

**Majority Opinion from* Brown v. Board of Education, *Federal Archives 347 U.S. 483 (1954).*
†*http://odur.let.rug.nl/~usa/D/1951-1976/integration/brown_i.htm*

good law school, and for the first time the Court ordered a black student admitted into a previously all-white school.

The opinion gave the NAACP and its chief legal counsel, Thurgood Marshall, the hope that the justices were finally ready to tackle the basic question of whether segregated facilities could ever in fact be equal. In 1952 the NAACP brought five cases before the Court specifically challenging the doctrine of *Plessy v. Ferguson*. The issue that had hung fire ever since the Civil War now had to be faced directly: what place would African Americans enjoy in the American polity?

A number of reports indicate that the justices, while agreed that segregation was wrong, were divided over whether the Court had the power to overrule *Plessy*. They therefore set the cases down for reargument in 1953, specifically asking both sides to address particular issues. Then Chief Justice Vinson, who reportedly opposed reversing *Plessy*, unexpectedly died a few weeks before the reargument, and the new chief justice, Earl Warren, skillfully steered the Court to its unanimous and historic ruling on May 17, 1954.

There is no question that the ruling in *Brown v. Board of Education*, which struck down racially enforced school segregation, is one of the most important in American history. No nation committed to democracy could hope to achieve those ideals while keeping people of color in a legally imposed position of inferiority. But the decision also raised a number of questions about the authority of the Court and whether this opinion represents a judicial activism that, despite its inherently moral and democratic ruling, is nonetheless an abuse of judicial authority. Other critics have pointed to what they claim is a lack of judicial neutrality or an overreliance on allegedly flawed social science findings.

But J. Harvie Wilkinson, who is now a federal circuit court judge, dismisses much of this criticism when he reminds us that Brown "was humane, among the most humane moments in all our history. It was ... a great political achievement, both in its uniting of the Court and in the steady way it addressed the nation."

With this decision, the nation picked up where it had left the cause of equal protection more than eighty years earlier, and began its efforts to integrate fully the black minority into full partnership in the American polity.

For further reading: Richard Kluger, *Simple Justice: The History of Brown v. Board of Education and Black America's Struggle for Equality* (1976); Mark Tushnet, *The NAACP's Strategy against Segregated Education, 1925–1950* (1987); and Daniel M. Berman, *It Is So Ordered: The Supreme Court Rules on School Segregation* (1966).

Brown v. Board of Education (1954)

Chief Justice Warren delivered the opinion of the Court.

These cases come to us from the States of Kansas, South Carolina, Virginia, and Delaware. In each of the cases, minors of the Negro race seek the aid of the courts in obtaining admission to the public schools of their community on a nonsegregated basis. In each instance, they had been denied admission to schools attended by white children under laws requiring or permitting segregation according to race. This segregation was alleged to deprive the plaintiffs of the equal protection of the laws under the 14th Amendment.... The plaintiffs contend that segregated public schools are not "equal" and cannot be made "equal," and that hence they are deprived of the equal protection of the laws. Argument was heard in the 1952 Term, and reargument was heard this Term on certain questions propounded by the Court.

Reargument was largely devoted to the circumstances surrounding the adoption of the 14th Amendment in 1868. It covered exhaustively consideration of the Amendment in Congress, ratification by the states, then existing practices in racial segregation, and the views of proponents and opponents of the Amendment. This discussion and our investigation convince us that, although these sources cast some light, it is not enough to resolve the problem with which we are faced. At best, they are inconclusive. The most avid proponents of the post–War Amendments undoubtedly intended them to remove all legal distinctions among "all persons born or naturalized in the United States." Their opponents, just as certainly, were antagonistic to both the letter and the spirit of the Amendments and wished them to have the most limited effect. What others in Congress and the state legislature had in mind cannot be determined with any degree of certainty.

An additional reason for the inconclusive nature of the Amendment's history, with respect to segregated schools, is the status of public education at that time. In the South, the movement toward free common schools, supported by general taxation, had not yet taken hold. Education of white children was largely in the hands of private groups. Education of Negroes was almost nonexistent, and practically all of the race were illiterate. In fact, any education of the Negroes was forbidden by law in some states. Today, in contrast, many Negroes have achieved outstanding success in the arts and sciences as well as in the business and professional world. It is true that public school education has advanced further in the North, but the effect of the Amendment on Northern States was generally ignored in the congressional debates. Even in the North, the conditions of public education did not approximate those existing today. The curriculum was usually rudimentary; ungraded schools were common in rural areas; the school term was but three months a year in many states; and compulsory school attendance was virtually unknown. As a consequence, it is not surprising that there should be so little in the history of the 14th Amendment relating to its intended effect on public education.

In the first cases in this Court construing the 14th Amendment, decided shortly after its adoption, the Court interpreted it as proscribing all state-imposed discriminations against the Negro race. The doctrine of "separate but equal" did not make its appearance in this Court until 1896, ... involving not education but transportation. In this Court, there have been six cases involving the "separate but equal" doctrine in the field of public education. In *Cumming v. County Board of Education* ... and *Gong Lum v. Rice,* ... the validity of the doctrine itself was not challenged. In more recent cases, all on the graduate school level, inequality was found in that specific benefits enjoyed by white students were denied to Negro students of the same educational qualifications.... In none of these cases was it necessary to reexamine the doctrine to grant relief to the Negro plaintiff. And in *Sweatt v. Painter* the Court expressly reserved decision on the question whether *Plessy v. Ferguson* should be held inapplicable to public education.

In the instant cases, that question is directly presented. Here, unlike *Sweatt v. Painter*, there are findings below that the Negro and white schools involved have been equalized or are being equalized, with respect to buildings, curricula, qualifications and salaries of teachers, and other "tangible" factors. Our decision, therefore, cannot turn on merely a comparison of these tangible factors in the Negro and white schools involved in each of the cases. We must look instead to the effect of segregation itself on public education.

In approaching this problem, we cannot turn the clock back to 1868 when the Amendment was adopted, or even to 1896 when *Plessy* was written. We must consider public education in the light of its full development and its present place in American life throughout the Nation. Only in this way can it be determined if segregation in public schools deprives these plaintiffs of the equal protection of the laws.

Today, education is perhaps the most important function of state and local governments. Compulsory school attendance laws and the great expenditures for education both demonstrate our recognition of the importance of education to our democratic society. It is required in the performance of our most basic public responsibilities, even service in the armed forces. It is the very foundation of good citizenship. Today it is a principle instrument in awakening the child to cultural values, in preparing him for later professional training, and in helping him to adjust normally to his environment. In these days, it is doubtful that any child may reasonably be expected to succeed in life if he is denied the opportunity of an education. Such an opportunity, where the state has undertaken to provide it, is a right which must be made available to all on equal terms.

We come then to the question presented: Does segregation of children in public schools solely on the basis of race, even though the physical facilities and other "tangible" factors may be equal, deprive the children of the minority group of equal educational opportunities? We believe that it does. In *Sweatt* in finding that a segregated law school for Negroes could not provide them equal educational opportunities, this Court relied in large part on "those qualities which are incapable of objective measurement but which make for greatness in a law school." In *McLaurin*, the Court, in requiring that a Negro admitted to a white graduate school be treated like all other students, again resorted to intangible considerations:

"[his] ability to study, to engage in discussions and exchange views with other students, and, in general, to learn his profession." Such considerations apply with added force to children in grade and high schools. To separate them from others of similar age and qualifications solely because of their race generates a feeling of inferiority as to their status in the community that may affect their heart and minds in a way unlikely ever to be undone. The effect of this separation on their educational opportunities was well stated by a finding in the Kansas case by a court which nevertheless felt compelled to rule against the Negro plaintiffs: "Segregation of white and colored children in public schools has a detrimental effect upon the colored children. The impact is greater when it has the sanction of the law; for the policy of separating the races is usually interpreted as denoting the inferiority of the negro group. A sense of inferiority affects the motivation of a child to learn. Segregation with the sanction of law, therefore, has a tendency to retard the educational and mental development of negro children and to deprive them of some of the benefits they would receive in a [racially] integrated school system." Whatever may have been the extent of psychological knowledge at the time of *Plessy v. Ferguson*, this finding is amply supported by modern authority. Any language in *Plessy v. Ferguson* contrary to this finding is rejected.

We conclude that in the field of public education the doctrine of "separate but equal" has no place. Separate educational facilities are inherently unequal. Therefore, we hold that the plaintiffs and others similarly situated for whom the actions have been brought are by reason of the segregation complained of, deprived of the equal protection of the laws guaranteed by the 14th Amendment. This disposition makes unnecessary any discussion whether such segregation also violates the Due Process Clause of the 14th Amendment.

Because these are class actions, because of the wide applicability of this decision, and because of the great variety of local conditions, the formulation of decrees in these cases presents problems of considerable complexity. On reargument, the consideration of appropriate relief was necessarily subordinated to the primary question — the constitutionality of segregation in public education. We have now announced that such segregation is a denial of the equal protection of the laws. In order that we may have the full assistance of the parties in formulating decrees, the cases will be restored to the docket, and the parties are requested to present further argument....

It is so ordered.

Appendix 3

United States District Judge
Frank A. Hooper Remarks, 1960*

IN THE UNITED STATES DISTRICT COURT
FOR THE NORTHERN DISTRICT OF GEORGIA

ATLANTA DIVISION
VIVIAN CALHOUN, et al.

v.

CITY OF ATLANTA, BOARD OF EDUCATION, et al.
CIVIL ACTION NO. 6298

Atlanta, Georgia; May 9, 1960

Before
His Honor FRANK A. HOOPER, Judge
Excerpt from remarks of Court

Appearances:

For Plaintiffs: Constance Baker Motley, E. E.
Moore Jr., Donald L. Hollowell, A. T. Walden

For Defendants: B. D. Murphy, Newell Edenfield, J. C. Savage

*Judge Frank A. Hooper's Remarks, Federal Archives, File 1, Box 55E.

THE COURT: I'm going to make a statement here. I'm not going to enter any order of Court this morning. It'll have to be entered later, and what I'm stating here will be only the basis for an opinion which I will write later. But I think that the people of our State here should know as soon as possible about the immediate situation. I'll take this statement which I'm making more or less off the cuff and edit it and write it in the form of a formal opinion.

I want to give a brief history of this particular case. This suit was filed and as far as I can tell the people of Georgia were rather complacent about this whole situation. My colleague, Judge Boyd Sloan and I therefore in the fall of 1958 passed an order advising that this case would be tried before September, 1959. Not until that order was signed and the people began to see that something would be done before September, 1959, did the public take any interest in it hardly at all. At that time, there were meetings held and various organizations were gotten together and this that and the other to attempt to try to save the public schools, particularly in Atlanta.

This Court had a hearing in June, 1959, in which it declared that segregation as practiced in the Atlanta School System was illegal and must cease. The Atlanta Board of Education was directed to make a plan and submit it by December, 1959; which was done. There were certain defects in that plan which the City very willingly rectified and changed as stated by Counsel a moment ago. The plan was finally approved I think January 18th of this year. I was asked by the Plaintiffs to put that plan into immediate effect, which would mean to be effective as of September, 1960. As the Georgia Legislature had appointed a committee to study this matter and it was composed of nineteen outstanding Georgians, I stated at that time that I would reserve a ruling until this date, May the 9th, and give the Legislative Committee an opportunity to make their report. I said that that would not delay the plan being effective in September, 1960, and neither has this postponement of the trial delayed it. I didn't mean by that that I was going to order the plan to be effective as of September, 1960. A great many people, including some newspaper writers, made that inference themselves; but I never did say that the plan would be effective as of September, 1960. 1 merely said that by having a hearing on May the 9th rather than in January as to when it starts, that that would not delay it. It has not delayed it.

I could on this date order the plan to be effective as of September, 1960, because under the plan those applying for transfers have until the 15th of this month. I assume they already have their applications fixed up and they could very quickly file them and still get them in before May the 15th. I have always said throughout this whole matter that I would consider the question of the starting time as of the time after this committee reported. That is, I said that as of the time when the committee was appointed.

Now I do not agree with those who have said that the appointment of this legislative committee was futile. Whether by appointing it the Legislature was hoping to get more time or not, I do not know. Maybe they were. But I do not think that the appointment of the committee was a useless act, nor do I think that it has not been without very substantial benefits.

The majority report here signed by the Chairman, Mr. John A. Sibley — I regret to hear that he was injured a few days ago in an automobile accident. I am told that it was not serious, of which I am very glad — but this majority report is quite lengthy and I will not go into the details of it, but it makes several recommendations here, some of which require a constitutional amendment and some of which do not. It recommends statutes in regard to tuition grants by the State to students who are not attending the public schools. It provides for teacher retirement and certain things requiring a vote of the people. But as just pointed out, there are two recommendations made which do not require a constitutional amendment, which the Georgia Legislature to be elected next September and convening next January may adopt if they see fit, and that is the pupil placement or pupil assignment law which the Board of Education has already adopted, and which this Court has approved.

If the Georgia Legislature will allow the people of Atlanta to put through such a plan, it would prevent the closing of Atlanta schools in September, 1961.

The other provision which the Georgia Legislature could adopt which might prevent the closing would be to allow the people of Atlanta to vote on the question as to whether they would rather close their schools entirely rather than to have any integration or not. I'm not concerned now with the proposed legislative acts which would have to be ratified by the people, but merely point those two out.

Now the report of this legislative committee, sometimes called the Sibley Committee on account of its Chairman, states this: That in their hearings over the State of Georgia, that three to two witnesses favor maintaining segregation even though — even at the cost of abolishing public schools. That in itself shows a very decided shift in the sentiment of the people of Georgia. Had you put that to a vote a year ago, you wouldn't have had three favoring the maintaining of segregation at any cost and two voting the other way. You probably would have had all five voting to maintain segregation at any cost. So there is very definitely an increase in the number of people in the State of Georgia who fear the damage to the public school system by virtue of being closed for one year. They fear that so much that while they do not favor integration at all, they would rather have integration under a reasonable plan — I think a reasonable plan, which has been approved by this Court, which Mrs. Motley, Counsel for the Plaintiffs, says is the mildest plan that she's seen adopted anywhere. Personally, I think the plan would be approved by the higher courts. I think it would. I could be mistaken. It would be a gradual and moderate integration if it is approved. It would not throw all of our system into chaos and to a certain closing at least. Now I think it's well known that in Georgia we have a different feeling in the populous areas, in the cities, large towns, than what we have in the strictly rural area. Our cities and towns feel that they can handle the matter satisfactorily on account of the residential patterns that exist; and as I have previously pointed out, in some of my opinions on this matter, a white school located in the center of a white section will predominantly or altogether be filled with whites. A colored school [is] in the middle of a colored section by the Negroes. However, in the rural areas of Georgia a more different situation exists because and the Negroes in different areas. The residential pattern is more or less scattered. There are a number of large, consolidated schools taking pupils from various areas, and these areas are the ones where there is some feeling at the present time that their preference would be to not to allow the

City of Atlanta to have any integration whatsoever, but rather to have their representatives in the Legislature to vote against anything that would give Atlanta relief and let the Atlanta schools close.

I call attention to the facts stated in this legislative report as to the dangers that are inherent in that kind of an attitude, where the opinion of a three-judge Federal Court in Virginia discussed all of that and ruled that if you close any schools, it's unfair to the taxpayers in those areas to have to pay taxes and yet not get any schools, and as a result the court there in Virginia passed a decree which in effect ordered the Norfolk School System to be reopened on an integrated basis and enjoined the State officials from continuing to operate other schools unless the Norfolk Schools were likewise opened. That's the danger which our friends out in the rural area, or a great many, have seemed to overlook.

This Court has pointed out before that a great many Southern States have already adopted pupil placement laws such as that which has been approved for Atlanta. They [did] not adopt pupil placement laws because they favored integration. They wanted segregation. I think I can safely say that at least for Mississippi, Alabama and South Carolina. And yet they passed these laws. They passed these laws so that if it came to the question of the Court ordering integration, they would have gradual integration and not a sudden, explosive integration. Now so far, the Georgia Legislature has not seen fit to pass any such law. I think that attitude is somewhat like a general that says he's not going to build up the fortifications around his army against an attack because he thinks that might invite the enemy to attack him. I don't think so. I think that if you may have to retreat, it's a good idea not to burn the bridges behind you. And I'm personally of the opinion that these other Southern States feel about integration the same way Georgia did, and were wise to put an escape there in case they ever needed it.

I want to make it clear too that of these nineteen outstanding people who signed this Sibley Report, all nineteen of them said that they were opposed to integration. They felt like that Georgia ought to be allowed to run like it has under a Supreme Court decision for the last eighty years under that decision, and ever since the State was founded, as far as segregation is concerned. Georgia about had time to get used to that practice ever since it was a State, and it's rather shocking to try to change over to any other basis. But the fact that so many people in our State now favor gradual or token integration as it's sometimes called rather than closing the schools shows there has been a great shift in the sentiment of the people, even those who are more or less vigorously opposed to any integration whatsoever. The majority of the members of this committee here said they favored segregation, but it's something they can't do anything about. I might say it's any harbor in a storm, or it's a question not of what you would like, but of what is inevitable. And if a storm comes you want a storm cellar. You certainly did not create the storm or want the storm, but you want a storm cellar if it comes, and I take that to be more or less the attitude of a lot of people in our State. Now that's one thing the Legislature could do, of course, without any constitutional amendment.

Now as was pointed out a moment ago, those gentlemen that signed the minority report, they are also outstanding citizens of this State. They do not go along with the majority or their recommendations, but I think the minority impliedly recognized the situation in which we are placed. Paragraph 4 of their report is, quote, that the Governor and the General Assembly of Georgia take such action and enact such measures as may be required from time to time consistent with the welfare and best interest of the children of Georgia, end quote, and it could well be that a great many people in the Legislature would vote to have some integration or a gradual plan rather than a closing of all the schools in Georgia, because a great many citizens in the State of Georgia and mothers and fathers that are not financially able to afford the luxury of a private school, they would rather have some integration than to have the schools to close and be thrown on their own resources as to educating their children.

Now there is another thing I think is very important. The last Legislature which convened in January, 1960, were made up of men who as I said a moment ago almost without exception ran on a platform of no integration whatsoever. Since they were elected on that platform, a great many things have happened. We have had things to happen in Arkansas and we have had things to happen in Virginia. Next September, there'll be a great many other men running for the Legislature, Georgia Assembly, which is to meet in January, 1961. If those candidates for the Legislature who run in September and who'll convene in January go further than this minority report here of the Sibley Committee, they may find themselves in position that they got to vote against any give at all on the Atlanta situation, and force the closing of all the Georgia schools, even though at that time they may not think that's the best thing to do because they made promises to their constituents.

I want to make it clear that this Court's not trying to dabble into the affairs of the Legislature or any State official of the State of Georgia, but trying to be as helpful as possible. Neither is this Court trying to contrive for the people of Georgia some machinery whereby the decision of the U.S. Supreme Court can be evaded because I don't think we can evade it. The only thing this Court has been trying to do is to give the Georgia Legislature an opportunity of passing some law which — or plan — which has already been approved by the courts, the Supreme Court or a Circuit Court of Appeals which will permit the people of Georgia when integration comes by order of the Court of operating under some gradual plan rather than having the whole school system thrown into chaos and all closing and our school teachers all going away. And I have been careful not to try to make any direful predictions or anything of that sort because I don't know what will happen. But we have some inkling of that by what's happened in other states. Georgia may not have learned anything from Arkansas or Virginia. They may prefer even to wait as long as Virginia did until many, many thousands of children were out of school before they did anything at all. Some philosopher says that the one thing people learn from history is that you don't learn anything from history, and maybe Georgia is the same way. I don't know. I believe, though that with the leadership which has been furnished here by this Legislative Committee that Georgia might change its mind by next January. They might see fit to allow Atlanta to handle its own problem here and have some integration rather than to risk the dam breaking and the whole State being flooded.

Now this Legislative Committee I think was very carefully chosen. They are not people whose opinions should be treated lightly. You have here as a chairman one of Georgia's leading lawyers and bankers, and you have the General Counsel of that majority an able lawyer who has served with distinction in the Georgia Legislature, being a Senator. You have the chief people in Georgia who are interested in education and in keeping our schools open. Mr. Robert O. Arnold, Chairman of the Board of Regents; has charge of all the Georgia educational institutions on a higher level. You have Chancellor Harmon W. Caldwell, Chancellor of the University System. You have Doctor Claude Purcell, the Superintendent of Schools of the State of Georgia. And you have others there who have been named who are outstanding people, Senator Greer; Judge Boykin; Mr. Charles A. Cowan, President of the Georgia Municipal Association; Mr. Dent, President of Georgia State Chamber of Commerce; Mr. Kennimer, the head of the Georgia Education Association; Mr. Homer Rankin, President of the Georgia Press Association. I hope I haven't left any of them out. But all of those leaders of Georgia are vitally interested in education and they all pointed out the dangers we face and the fact that we had better do something about it. And yet every one of them said that they are not in favor of integration. They are in favor of keeping our system like it always has been. They point out what they think we had better do as against today. It might be dangerous to do otherwise.

Now in regard to the minority, these gentlemen see it differently. They say they want segregation. Well, so did the other group. They say that they want a guarantee that no Georgia child shall be forced against the desire of his parent or guardian to attend any public school where a child of the opposite race is enrolled. By that they refer to what's known as the freedom of choice plan which Virginia has adopted. I take it the majority doesn't differ with them on that. They say that second, they favor such legislation as may give grants in aid to children whose schools are integrated and where they wish to go somewhere else. I think maybe the majority agrees with that. I think a great many of our people do. Third, they favor the public school system being preserved on a segregated basis as far as it is possible to do so unless closed by unprecedented — by Federal Court decree. I don't think the majority would differ with them on that. The significant thing is, though, that the minority as I said before recommend that the Governor and General Assembly of Georgia take such action as may be required consistent with the welfare and best interests of the children of Georgia, and that is the thing on which this Court pins its hopes, that the Legislature in January, 1961, will do. If not, it's the last chance and it is the last chance that this Court, I think, I can give to the Legislature and people of Georgia to avoid what may come.

Therefore this Court is of [the] opinion that to order the Atlanta Public Schools to integrate under the plan as made in September, 1960, could mean but one thing: That is, the closing of Atlanta schools. That to postpone this until — to be effective as of May 1, 1961, will give the Georgia Legislature, a newly elected Legislature, an uncommitted Legislature just one chance to prevent this closing. However, under the present plan which the Court has approved, only the 12th grade was to be made subject to that plan, and applications for transfer assignments were to be made to the 12th grade. And I am — will in my order provide that next year, that would be made applicable not only to the 12th but to the 11th grade, and that means that by deferring the start of this plan until September, '61, instead of September, '60, the completion of the plan will be on exactly the same date as though it had started at this time.

This statement that I have made, Ladies and Gentlemen, as I say is largely off the cuff, and I will have to edit it and put it in the form of a written opinion and an order of the Court.

Appendix 4

Majority and Minority Reports of the Georgia General Assembly Committee on Schools, 1960*

The Majority Report of the General Assembly Committee on Schools

I. The Background

In the 1896 case of *Plessy v. Ferguson*, 163 U.S. 537 (1896), the U.S. Supreme Court held that "separate but equal" facilities met the requirements of the Fourteenth Amendment that no state should deprive its citizens of the "equal protection of the laws." At least eight subsequent Supreme Court decisions and more than 70 lower federal and state court cases followed that doctrine. In reliance on that doctrine many billions of dollars have been spent to make the separate schools for Negroes truly equal in all respects to those provided for white children.

At one time or another, after the adoption of the amendment, 23 states maintained segregated schools by law, including New York, Illinois, California, and Kansas among other non-southern states.

*Majority and Minority Reports from the Georgia General Assembly Committee on Schools, John Sibley Papers, Manuscript, Archives and Rare Book Library, Emory University.

In 1954 with no change in the Constitution and no congressional legislation, the Supreme Court held that separate schools, regardless of the quality of their facilities, personnel and program, are inherently unequal and therefore unconstitutional. *Brown v. Board of Education of Topeka,* 347 U.S. 483 (1954).

We consider this decision utterly unsound on the facts; contrary to the clear intent of the Fourteenth Amendment; a usurpation of legislative function through judicial process; and an invasion of the reserved rights of states. We further consider that, putting aside the question of segregation, this decision represents a clear and present danger to our system of constitutional government, because it places what the court calls "modern authority" in sociology and psychology above the ancient authority of the law, and because it places the transitory views of the Supreme Court above the legislative power of Congress, the settled construction of the Constitution, and the reserved sovereignty of the several states.

Nevertheless, we must recognize that the decision exists: that it is binding on the lower federal courts; and that it will be enforced.

II. General Assembly Committee on Schools

Because of a pending suit in a federal court to bring about the integration of the races in the Atlanta school system, the General Assembly of Georgia at its 1960 session expressed the belief "that the people of Georgia may wish to make a deliberate determination as to whether future education is to be afforded through direct tuition payments for use in private schools devoid of governmental control, or whether the public school system as it presently exists shall be maintained notwithstanding that the school system of Atlanta and even others yet to come may be integrated."

In order that the General Assembly might be in a better position to make a determination as to the wisdom of presenting this question to the people, "the Assembly felt that it should have the advice and counsel of the people, not only as to the desirability of the presentation, but also as to its form and content."

As a means of obtaining expressions of opinion from the people, the General Assembly created the General Assembly Committee on Schools consisting of nineteen members. This Committee was directed, immediately upon the adjournment of the General Assembly, to conduct at least one public hearing in each congressional district of the state.

The Committee was directed to make positive recommendations to the General Assembly "regarding whether or not to submit the question to the people of Georgia for their determination," and in the event the Committee should recommend the submission of the question to the people, the Committee was asked to recommend "the time, manner and form of the submission, including its contents." The Committee was also directed to "make such other and further recommendations as it may deem proper."

The Committee held the hearings as directed. It received testimony from more than 1,800 witnesses, representing or purporting to represent more than 115,000 people. Among these witnesses were more than 1,600 white persons and 200 Negroes. In addition the Committee has received over 600 letters from individuals and petitions bearing more than 6,000 signatures. A three to two majority of the witnesses favored maintaining segregation even at the cost of abolishing public schools. The hearings disclosed a nearly unanimous feeling on basic principles regarding segregation and public schools, but a wide difference of opinion on the course of that should be taken to meet the situation created by the federal court decision.

The testimony cannot be accurately assessed as to the mathematical proportion of the people of Georgia holding particular opinions, because of the defects inherent in the only procedures that the committee could adopt and because of the comparatively small number of the people who could be heard. For example, 40 per cent of the counties were represented by three or fewer witnesses. Nevertheless, the committee has been able to reach these conclusions, based on the testimony presented to it:

1. An overwhelming majority of people in Georgia have a deep conviction that separate school facilities for the white and colored races are in the best interest of both races, and that compulsory association of the races in the schools through enforced integration will be detrimental to the peace, good order and tranquility of the state and to the progress,

harmony and good relations between the races. With this opinion your committee is in full agreement.

2. The vast majority of the people prefer tax-supported, segregated public schools rather than private schools with or without grants in aid from the state. It is their belief that it is in the public schools that the youth of the state receive training for the responsibilities of citizenship in a democracy; that to close the public schools and go to a system of private schools even with such grants in aid would make it more difficult for many young people to obtain an adequate education. The burden would be particularly heavy on those in the lower income brackets. With these views your committee is also in full accord.

3. Testimony received by the committee indicated that if total segregation cannot be maintained in a state-wide system of public schools, there is no unanimity of opinion as to the course that should be followed. Three points of view are expressed:

(a) A large number of people are willing to close the schools on a statewide basis, rather than allow any integration anywhere.

(b) A large number of people desire that the choice between closing the schools and accepting integration be left to the community affected. This viewpoint is predicated on two considerations: First, many people, believing that their own school systems will not be confronted with integration problems within the foreseeable future, are unwilling to sacrifice their schools to maintain segregation in other parts of the state; and second, a number of people feel that conditions are so varied throughout the state that the decisions on local problems should be left to local authorities.

(c) A large number of people though believing in the desirability of segregation, would be willing to accept some degree of integration rather than to sacrifice their public schools.

III. The Present Legal Situation

If a Negro child is ordered into a white Atlanta school, the governor is required, under 1955 and 1956 laws (Code 32–801, et seq.) to close all the schools in the Atlanta system. Expenditures of state or local funds to operate an integrated school system are prohibited and made a felony, and personal civil liability is imposed on those making such expenditures.

Other Georgia laws also prohibit the support of integrated schools by state or local tax funds. Among them are these:

The Georgia Constitution requires that "Separate schools shall be provided for the white and colored races" (Code 2–6401); the 1956 appropriation act (Ga. Laws 1956, p. 753, 758) under which the state is still operating, provides that funds are cut off for school districts ordered desegregated; a 1955 act (Code 32–802) requires that budgets submitted by local school districts to the State Board of Education provide that the funds therein requisitioned will lapse in the event of integration.

If any Atlanta school is closed, no other school district is necessarily affected. However, when the same situation arose in Norfolk, Virginia, parents of white children who had attended the closed schools brought suit and a three-judge federal court held:

"Tested by these principles we arrive at the inescapable conclusion that the Commonwealth of Virginia, having accepted and assumed the responsibility of maintaining and operating public schools, cannot act through one of its Officers to close one or more public schools in the state solely by reason of the assignment to, or enrollment or presence in that public school of children of different races or colors, and, at the same time, keep other public schools throughout the state open on a segregated basis. The 'equal protection' afforded to all citizens and taxpayers is lacking in such a situation. While the State of Virginia, directly or indirectly, maintains and operates a school system with the use of public funds, or participates by arrangement or otherwise in the management of such a school system, no one public school or grade in Virginia may be closed to avoid the effect of the law of the land as interpreted by the Supreme Court, while the state permits other public schools or grades to remain open at the expense of the taxpayers." —*James v. Almond*, 170 F. Supp. 331.

The decree based upon this decision ordered that the Norfolk schools be reopened on an integrated basis, and enjoined the state officials from continuing to operate other schools unless the Norfolk schools were likewise open. The decree did not order or contemplate closing all the schools of the state, and the state did not undertake closing the statewide school system; instead it decided to accept integration in Norfolk and subsequently in other areas.

It must be assumed that a similar suit would be filed by Atlanta parents, and that a similar holding would follow, although the committee cannot undertake to predict the form which the decree effectuating such a holding would take.

In any event, under such a holding the state would be faced with the necessity for deciding whether to close all the schools of the state, by legislation or otherwise, or to accept integration of the Atlanta schools.

IV. Freedom of Choice

The Constitution of the United States, as interpreted by the Supreme Court, is controlling and binding upon the courts and the people; and the state laws, insofar as they are in conflict with the federal law, are unenforceable.

Any system of public education must now recognize that the Supreme Court decision in the Brown case destroyed the power of the state to compel by law separation of the races in public, tax-supported schools. Any continuance of public education must be adjusted to that fact.

It is important, therefore, to determine the scope and limitations of the *Brown* case as interpreted and applied by the federal courts. We quote from the decisions as follows:

> Desegregation does not mean that there must be intermingling of the races in all school districts. It means only that they may not be prevented from intermingling or going to school together because of race or color.
>
> If it is a fact, as we understand it is, with respect to Buchanan School, that the district is inhabited entirely by colored students, no violation of any constitutional right results because they are compelled to attend the school in the district in which they live. *Brown v. Board of Education of Topeka Kansas*, 139 F. Supp. 468 (D. C. Kan. 1955)

(This was a later decision in the *Brown* case, rendered after the case went back to the District Court for implementation.)

> Having said this, it is important that we point out exactly what the Supreme Court has decided and what it has not decided in this case. It has not decided that the Federal Courts are to take over or regulate the public schools of the states. It has not decided that the states must mix persons of

different races in the schools or must require them to attend school or must deprive them of the right of choosing the school they attend. What it has decided, and all that it has decided, is that a state may not deny to any person on account of race the right to attend any school that it maintains. This, under the decision of the Supreme Court, the state may not do directly or indirectly; but if the schools in which it maintains are open to children of all races, no violation of the Constitution is involved even though the children of different rates voluntarily attend different schools, as they attend different churches. Nothing in the Constitution or in the decision of the Supreme Court takes away from the people freedom to choose the schools they attend. The Constitution in other words, does not require integration. It merely forbids discrimination. It does not forbid such segregation as occurs as the result of voluntary action. It merely forbids the use of governmental power to enforce segregation. The Fourteenth Amendment is a limitation upon the exercise of power by the state or state agencies, not a limitation upon the freedom of individuals. *Briggs v. Elliott*, 132 F. Supp. 776 (D. C. S. C. 1955)

The Constitution as construed in the School Segregation Cases; *Brown v. Board of Education*, forbids any state action requiring segregation of children in public schools solely on account of race; it does not however, require actual integration of the races. (Court then quoted from *Briggs* case, quoted herein above.) *Avery v. Wichita Falls Independent School District*, 241 F2d 230 (C. A. 5th 1957), cert. den. 353 U. S. 938.

It must be remembered that the decisions of the Supreme Court of the United States in *Brown v. Board of Education* do not compel the mixing of the different races in the public schools. No general reshuffling of the pupils in any school system has been commanded. The order of that court is simply that no child shall be denied admission to a school on the basis of race or color. Indeed, just so a child is not through any form of compulsion or pressure required to stay in a certain school, or denied transfer to another school, because of his race or color, the school heads may allow the pupil, whether white or Negro, to go to the same school as he would have attended in the absence of the ruling of the Supreme Court. Consequently, compliance with that ruling may well not necessitate such extensive changes in the school system as some anticipate. *Thompson v. School Board of Arlington*, 144 F. Supp. 239

(D. C. Va. 1956), affirmed sub nom. *School Board of Charlottesville v. Allen*, 240 F2d 59 (C. A. 4th 1956), cert. den. 77 S. Ct. 667 (2 cases).

The equal protection and due process clauses of the Fourteenth Amendment do not affirmatively command integration, but they do forbid any state action requiring segregation on account of race or color of children in the public schools. *Avery v. Wichita Falls Indep. School District*, 5 Cir, 1957, 241 F2d 230, 233.

Pupils may, of course, be separated according to their degree of advancement or retardation, their ability to learn, on account of their health, or for any other legitimate reason, but each child is entitled to be treated as an individual without regard to his race or color. *Borders v. Rippy*, 247 F2d 268 (C. A. 5th 1957).

In *Plessy v. Ferguson*, which was good law for sixty-eight years until superseded by the *Brown* case, the Supreme Court very wisely recognized that compulsory association can only bring about the tensions and social disorder which have resulted from the 1954 decision:

If the two races are to meet upon terms of social equality, it must be the result of natural affinities, a mutual appreciation of each other's merits, and a voluntary consent of individuals. As was said by the Court of Appeals of New York in *People v. Gallagher*, 93 N. Y, 438, 448: "This end can neither be accomplished nor promoted by laws which conflict with the general sentiment of the community upon whom they are designed to operate. When the government, therefore, has secured to each of its citizens equal rights before the law, and equal opportunities for improvement and progress, it has accomplished the end for which it was organized, and performed all of the functions respecting social advantages with which it is endowed." Legislation is powerless to eradicate racial instincts, or to abolish distinctions based upon physical differences, and the attempt to do so can only result in accentuating the difficulties of the present situation. If the civil and political rights of both races be equal, one cannot be inferior to the other civilly or politically. If one race be inferior to the other socially, the Constitution of the United States cannot put them upon the same plane. *Plessy v. Ferguson*, 163 U.S. 537 (1896).

Thus it is seen that while the state is without power to enforce racial segregation in schools by law, the federal government under the Constitution is without power to impose integration upon the individual. As was pointed out by the Court in the *Briggs* case above, "nothing in the Constitution or in the decision of the Supreme Court takes away from the people freedom to choose the schools they attend. The Constitution ... does not require integration." The state therefore may within the bounds of the federal constitution establish a system of public education that preserves and guarantees this freedom of choice to the individual — the right of the individual to select his own associates.

This right is especially valuable during the impressionable and formative school age. The educational process is as much a social matter as an intellectual one, and the parent has the right and the duty to place his child in a school where an atmosphere of harmony and congeniality prevails and where the child can work with acceptable companions toward the attainment of their common educational goals. The parent has the responsibility to avoid the selection of a school with an atmosphere of compulsory and undesirable associations and where there exist the contentions and hostilities that so often result from the strife of judicial proceedings and court orders.

This right of free choice of one's associates is in violation of no law, state or federal, and is sanctioned by all enlightened people. It is the foundation stone of all society and is the base upon which progress, happiness, good order and good feeling among people are built.

The United States Supreme Court has very recently held that freedom of association is embraced within the First Amendment guarantees against governmental encroachment. *N.A.A.C.P. v. Alabama*, 357 U.S. 449 (1958); *Bates v. Little Rock*, 4 L. Ed. 2d 480, 485 (1960). The freedom to associate necessarily implies the freedom not to associate.

The question before the Committee is whether the people of Georgia should be permitted to say whether they desire to establish a system of' public schools within the framework of the federal court decisions, with such safeguards as will protect the right of free choice of both the parent of the child and of the local community, and that will guarantee that no child in Georgia will be compelled to go to a mixed school against the wishes of his parent or guardian.

When Georgia in 1954 amended its constitution so as to make possible tuition grants from public funds to enable students to attend private schools, the plan offered what then seemed to be an effective alternative to mixed schools. These grants were to be in lieu of all other educational responsibility of the state, and it was assumed that schools could be closed on a system-by-system basis as they became subject to federal court decrees, and that tuition grants would be made available to each such system only upon the event of its closing. It was not contemplated that a situation would come about wherein the state could legally close its schools only on a statewide basis. That situation has developed because of later decisions by the federal courts. The Amendment, however, in permitting grants in aid, was a farsighted act of statesmanship and, regardless of the turn of events, can be of great help in working out a solution of the present problem.

V. Conclusions

The conclusion is inescapable that to maintain total segregation everywhere in the state, the state will almost certainly have to withdraw from the operation of public schools. Presumably, under the 1954 amendment to the Georgia Constitution (Code 2–7502), the state could give grants or scholarships to individual school children for use in such private schools as may exist or may be established. The state could have nothing to do with the organization, operation, or supervision of such private schools. "State support of segregated schools through any arrangement, management, funds or property cannot be squared with the Amendment's command that no state shall deny to any person within its jurisdiction the equal protection of the laws." *Cooper v. Aaron*, 358 U.S. 1 (1958).

Leasing publicly owned facilities to private operators to avoid integration has been held invalid. *Aaron v. Cooper*, 261 F. 2d 97 (C.A. 8th 1958), and cases cited at page 108. Hence, existing public school buildings, buses, books and the like could not be used except after a bona fide purchase by private schools at fair market value.

There are many other serious and difficult problems involved in the establishment and operation of private schools. Among them is the provision of adequate funds for the many phases of school operations. Building must be financed, transportation facilities must be secured, adequate funds for operation must be found. The problems of accreditation for the private schools will demand serious study. The costs per student are likely to be so high that many students will be unable to attend because any possible tuition grants will be inadequate to cover the costs. And perhaps most serious of all is the fact that a democratic state will lose all control over the institutions in which the minds, character and ideals of the future citizens of the state are molded.

It is our conclusion that, although there are some localities where such private schools could be maintained successfully, it will be impractical to develop a system of private schools that will provide adequately for the educational needs of the masses of the people of the state.

Furthermore, even if a system of private schools is adopted, the state, having no control of such schools would be powerless to prohibit integration in them if some private schools voluntarily integrated. Those who want to mix voluntarily can mix under the law and the state is powerless to prevent it.

The basic alternative to closing the public schools and turning to private schools or accepting integration by court order appears to be a system giving authority to local boards to assign students to particular schools in accordance with the best interests of all students; and the giving of as much freedom of choice as possible to parents and local communities in the handling of their problems; and the giving of assurance that no child will be required to go to school with a child of a different race except on a voluntary basis.

Under a pupil placement plan, the board of each school district, or the governing authority of a school administrative unit, in making assignments of students to particular schools, may properly consider the place of residence of the student, his level of intelligence, his educational attainments, his home environment, his physical condition, and any other facts and circumstances that may bear on the question of the student's ability and fitness to do successful work in a particular school and to maintain satisfactory relationships with those with whom he will be associated, but without reference to race or color.

As stated by Judge Hooper in the Atlanta case:

> Essentially the Plan contemplates that all pupils in the school shall, until and unless transferred to some other school, remain where they are; all new and beginning students being assigned by the Superintendent or his authority, to a school selected by observance of certain standards as set forth in the Proposed Plan.

Later Judge Hooper states:

> A general review of the measures taken in many southern states and border states since the rendition of the *Brown* decision, "both by way of legislative enactments and by way of plans adopted without legislative action show that

the so-called Pupil Placement Plan (also referred to as Pupil Assignment Plans, Enrollment Plans, etc.) have been adopted in one form or another in many states, including Virginia, North Carolina, Alabama, Louisiana, South Carolina, Florida, and Tennessee. In some of these states the plans were adopted soon after the *Brown* decision, although there was at the time of the adoption of the same no litigation pending nor any action being taken toward the elimination of racial discrimination. The plans were no doubt adopted against the day when such efforts would be made and they were adopted in full recognition of the fact that the people of the states adopting them had no desire to abolish segregation, but considered it wise to make plans for the future against the day when segregation in such states might be enjoined by the courts. Mississippi was one of the first states to adopt such legislation, though as yet there have been no efforts to abolish segregation in that state.

Similar plans have been held valid by the federal courts. *Shuttlesworth v. Birmingham Bd. of Educ.*, 358 U.S. 101 (1958); *Parham v. Dove*, 271 F 2d 132 (C.A. 8th 1959); *Covington v. Edwards*, 264 F 2d 780 (C.A. 4th 1959).

A provision permitting each school district confronted with an unsatisfactory situation, to determine for itself whether to close its schools, would give each community the maximum freedom of choice. It is assumed that such a Provision would also allow subsequent action by the school district to alter the original decision; that is the community could decide from time to time whether it wished to reopen closed schools or to close integrated ones. The validity of such a provision has not been tested in the courts but in the light of many analogous situations it should be upheld. Such provisions are in effect in other states.

The evidence shows that public school problems throughout the state are infinitely varied. A plan giving to each local community the right to determine its own course of action on problems of a peculiarly local nature appears to offer the best and most democratic procedure for solving these peculiarly local problems.

A provision permitting each parent to withdraw his child from an integrated school and to have the child assigned to a nonintegrated school, if one is available, or else given a tuition grant for private schooling appears to provide the maximum freedom of choice to each parent. The right of a parent to choose between public and private schools has never been questioned; in fact, such a right has been expressly upheld by the Supreme Court. *Pierce v. Society of Sisters*, 268 U.S. 510, (1925). It is difficult to see how a plan of tuition grants, available to all parents who desire private education for their children could be challenged successfully.

If the schools are to be closed, the step should be taken as a deliberate choice, with the expectation that the state will go out of the school business permanently, except for providing tuition grants or scholarships and that the people will resort to private schools. Closing the schools otherwise is a useless gesture and can cause nothing but confusion, great economic loss, and utter chaos in the administration of the school system.

It should also be borne in mind that whatever the final decision may be as to the course of action to be followed, there will be far greater mobility and flexibility in the handling of local school situations, if the choice of the course of action can be made freely at the local level rather than under the compulsion of a court order. It has been abundantly demonstrated in other jurisdictions that the federal courts do not hesitate to strike down, as attempts to circumvent their orders, statutes or practices which might have been approved as valid if taken voluntarily.

Those who insist upon total segregation must face the fact that it cannot be maintained in public schools by state law. If they insist upon total segregation everywhere in the state they must be prepared to accept eventual abandonment of public education.

Those who insist upon total segregation, but who back away from closing the schools, are not only deceiving themselves and the people, but are creating a very difficult and harmful situation: if the State stands upon the present laws, yet declines to accept the ultimate closing of the schools, the result will be integration in its worst form: coercive integration by court order, with no safeguards available to the local people and no freedom of action on the part of the parents of children affected.

The alternative is to establish a system of education within the limitations of the Supreme Court decision, yet one which will secure the maximum segregation possible within the law, which will vest the control of its schools in the people of the community, and which will ensure the parent the greatest freedom in protecting the welfare of his child.

To put this alternative into effect, the Committee believes that some changes are necessary in the Georgia Constitution. The guaranty that no child should be required to attend school with a child of another race ought to be one of the fundamental rights protected by the Constitution. The provision for local control of schools probably requires Constitutional authority vested in the General Assembly. There is no authority in law for a purely advisory referendum, and under a representative form of government. Any such referendum could not properly be made binding on the General Assembly.

Since any Constitutional amendment requires ratification by a vote of the people in a general election, this would provide the opportunity for the people to determine for themselves the course which they desire to take. The complex details of the necessary statutes are a responsibility of the General Assembly and could be developed practicably only through the legislative process.

VI. The Recommendation

The Committee recognizes, as has been heretofore stated, the people of Georgia, though overwhelmingly in favor of both segregation and public schools, are widely divided as to the best means of meeting the situation that confronts them; that the question profoundly affects every phase of the future life and activities of the people of the state; that the question should be considered in an atmosphere of calmness and far-sighted wisdom; that the question should be decided only after the most careful deliberation and the most thoughtful consideration of all the issues involved; and that the public school system is of such transcendent importance that its fate ought to be decided by a direct vote of the people. The people of Georgia have never been called upon to make a more important decision.

The Committee further recognizes that the primary concern of each Georgia citizen is the welfare of his own children and that regardless of the fate of the public schools, each parent should be protected by the Georgia constitution from being forced to allow his child to attend a school under what the parent considers intolerable circumstances.

The Committee further recognizes that the situation before it is one subject to unforeseen future developments and that the Legislature should have the maximum latitude in meeting such developments, including certain constitutional powers which it does not now possess.

We Therefore Recommend:

1. That the General Assembly propose to the people of Georgia an amendment to the Constitution, reading substantially as follows:

Notwithstanding any other provision in this Constitution, no child of this state shall be compelled against the will of his or her parent or guardian, to attend the public schools with a child of the opposite race; that any child whose parent or guardian objects to his attending an integrated school, shall be entitled to reassignment, if practicable, to another public school, or shall be entitled to a direct tuition grant or scholarship aid, as provided by this Constitution and as may be authorized by the General Assembly.

2. That the General Assembly propose to the people of Georgia a further amendment to the Constitution substantially as follows:

Notwithstanding any other provision of this Constitution, the General Assembly may provide for a uniform system of local units for the administration of the schools and authorize any such local administration unit, as defined by the General Assembly, to close schools within the unit or to reopen the schools in accordance with the wishes of a majority of the qualified voters of the unit as expressed in a formal election called for the purpose of ascertaining the wishes of the voters.

3. That the General Assembly forthwith enact legislation providing for tuition grants or scholarships for the benefit of any child whose parent chooses to withdraw said child from an integrated school and for the benefit of any child whose school has been closed, whether as a result of existing or future Georgia laws or as a result of a court order.

4. That the General Assembly forthwith enact legislation making the existing teacher retirement system available to teachers in private schools in the same manner and on the same basis as it now extends to teachers in public schools.

5. That the General Assembly consider, whether, in view of the urgency created by the Atlanta case and other cases which may be brought, it will propose to close the public schools in order to maintain total segregation throughout the state or whether it will choose a course designed to keep the schools open with as much freedom of choice to each parent

and community as possible; and, if it chooses the latter course, that it enact legislation enabling each school board or other local body to establish a pupil assignment plan; empowering the people of each community to vote whether to close their schools in the event of integration or to continue the operation of said schools, and enabling each parent to withdraw his child from an integrated school and have the child reassigned to a segregated school or receive a tuition grant or scholarship for private education.

The General Assembly Committee on Schools: John A. Sibley, Chairman Howell Hollis, General Counsel; John W. Greer, Secretary; Robert O. Arnold, Samuel J. Boykin, Harmon W. Cardwell, Charles A. Cowan, John W. Dent, Zade Kenimer, Dr. Claude Purcell, Homer Rankin.

The Minority Report of the General Assembly Committee on Schools

The General Assembly did not cast us adrift on an unchartered sea of deliberation without any semblance of a plotted course to guide our processes of decision. The General Assembly was not concerned with our individual opinions on the issues presented. If an independent judgment unaffected by the forces of external public opinion were all that had been called for, the lawmakers could have made such a determination for themselves, and there would have been no occasion for a fact finding tribunal. Instead, the Legislature stated its believe that "the people of *Georgia* may wish to make a deliberate determination...," and we were explicitly directed to hold "public hearings" and receive evidence "on the subject of maintaining public schools in Georgia in light of the order and judgment of Judge Hooper, or whether the *people prefer* a system of direct tuition grants" (Emphasis supplied). The requirement by law of a hearing carries with it by implication the additional requirement that whatever decision is reached must be based on the evidence received at such hearing, *I.C.C. v. L & N Railroad Co.,* 227 U. S. 88 (913), and any finding completely contrary to the evidence so adduced is erroneous, and constitutes a denial of the process. *Thompson v. Louisville,* 4 L. Ed. 2d 654 (1960).

The Committee has held its hearings and received evidence in the form of personal testimony and written communication. The people having spoken in such unmistakable language, it is nothing less than an intolerable affectation of superior virtue for us now to proclaim to them, "Well, not withstanding that you have made clear your sentiments, we think that you are wrong and that we know what is best for you."

As a result of the hearings held, we find virtually unanimous sentiment among the people of this State of all races that continued maintenance of separate education is in the best interests of all our citizens.

We find further, upon considering all evidence presented, that any precipitant action, resulting in enforced integration at this time in any community, would do incalculable harm to the children and would result in disastrous consequences which should and could be averted.

We find that enforced integration in the schools in this State would cause serious civil turmoil, bitterness, rancor, and internal strife, inflicting much harm on the people of Georgia and accomplishing nothing for the welfare of its citizens.

This Committee finds further that those who instituted, and those who control, the present school litigation in Georgia are not interested in the true well-being of either race, and are motivated by designs inconsistent with the further happiness and progress of the citizens of this State.

I
Responsibility of Committee

This Committee was created by the 1960 Session of the General Assembly to study the existing school problem in Georgia.

The General Assembly directed the Committee to hold hearings, at least one in each Congressional District of Georgia, to ascertain "whether future education is to be afforded through direct tuition payments for use in private schools devoid of governmental control, or whether the public school system as it presently exists shall be maintained notwithstanding that the school system of Atlanta and even others yet to come, may be integrated."

Said resolution creating this Committee further provides:

> The General Assembly Committee on Schools shall proceed immediately upon the adjournment of this session to hold public hearings under such rules and procedures as may be promulgated by the Committee, and after

ample notice thereof, to the extent of at least one hearing in each Congressional District of this State on the subject of maintaining public schools in Georgia in light of the order and judgment of Judge Hooper, or whether the people prefer a system of direct tuition grants under the Georgia Constitution for use in private schools, and that such suggestions as may be offered on or in modification of either course be received and considered, and that the Atlanta plan also be considered.

II
Results of Hearings

This Committee has conducted public hearings in eleven Georgia communities, at least one in each Congressional District. The results show that of all witnesses testifying 940 were for option No. 1 and 779 for option No. 2. The counties voted 91 for option No. 1 and 48 for option No. 2; 9 counties were evenly divided. Seven districts voted clearly for option No. 1, and three for option No. 2. All of these computations include both white and colored witnesses.

III
Pupil Placement or "Token Integration"

We believe that "pupil placement," "token integration," or "controlled desegregation" are one and the same.

Those who provoked the pending litigation in Georgia and elsewhere have publicly proclaimed unequivocal dissatisfaction with any plan short of massive and total integration on all levels. Many of the witnesses, both white and colored, representing the NAACP and other radical elements which appeared before the Committee expressed themselves to this effect. Several such witnesses specifically attached the Atlanta pupil placement plan as an illegal scheme designed to evade the Court's decision in the Brown case.

IV
Present Georgia Laws

The Constitution and laws of Georgia clearly do not envision, permit, provide, or authorize total school closings in Georgia in any circumstance. All persons who have read the law know this.

His Excellency, the Governor of Georgia, in a speech prepared for delivery before the Georgia Education Association on March 19, 1960, had this to say:

> As long as I am governor, Georgia children will continue to receive a good education by Georgia teachers.
>
> Lets give the lie once and for all to the canard that if one school in Georgia is integrated in Georgia, all the schools will close.
>
> The Georgia law simply does not authorize or contemplate massive school closings under any circumstances.
>
> We don't want to see even one school closed, and this will come about only as a last resort after all other measures have failed.
>
> The education of the children in that school would be provided for and the teachers would be taken care of and their retirement rights protected.

After a diligent search by responsible legal authorities and members of the Committee it was found that in no state has the result of litigation been the closing of all public schools.

Should any effort be made through any legal device or scheme to close all public schools of the State or to deny funds for their operation, the burden of responsibility must lie elsewhere than on the State Constitution, the State laws, State officials or the General Assembly.

The Committee as a whole has definitely concluded that it is the best interests of this State for the newspapers, the radio stations, the television stations, other information media, civic, fraternal, farm, labor, veteran, educational, business, professional, and all other groups and organizations in this State to exert every influence to maintain separation of the races in this State, and the public schools thereof, on a voluntary basis. If public opinion would unite to this end, we are certain that there would be no litigation in the first instance.

This Committee further deplores and condemns efforts on the part of Communist-inspired organizations who would do otherwise, and thus, inflict incalculable damage on the welfare and further happiness of the people of this State.

V
Recommendation

After due deliberation, and in full consideration of the facts as herein set forth, we recognize that it is difficult to formulate recommendations that would offer any perfect solution to the problem presented.

However, as the most effective means of dealing with the problem, we recommend that the General Assembly provide, either through the form of appropriate constitutional amendments, and/or through enactment of new statutes or amendments to the existing laws, measures which would accomplish the following purposes, to wit:

1. Guarantee that no Georgia child shall be forced against the desire of his parent or guardian to attend any public school wherein a child of the opposite race is enrolled.

2. That the General Assembly of Georgia, pursuant to the 1954 Amendment to the Georgia Constitution, as advocated and proposed by Honorable Herman E. Talmadge, then Governor of Georgia, enact such appropriate enabling legislation as may be required to further effectuate the grants-in-aid amendment so as to provide for direct grants of State, County, and Municipal Funds to citizens of the State for educational purposes, in discharge of all obligations of the State to provide adequate education for its citizens.

3. That the public school system be preserved on a segregated basis as far as it is possible to do so unless closed by unprecedented federal court decree, and that the system of grants be instituted only as a last resort.

4. That the Governor and the General Assembly of Georgia take such action and enact such measures as may be required from time to time, consistent with the welfare and best interests of the children of Georgia.

The General Assembly
Committee on Schools

John P. Duncan,
Vice-Chairman
George Brooks
J. Battle Hall
Render Hill

Wallace L. Jernigan

H. Walstein Parker
H. Eulond Clary
J. W. Keyton

Chapter Notes

Chapter 1

1. Lester Maddox. Pickwick's Restaurant Advertisement, *Atlanta Journal*, April 25, 1959.
2. Jeff Roche. *Restructured Resistance: The Sibley Commission and the Politics of Desegregation in Georgia*. Athens: The University of Georgia Press, 1998, 73.
3. Harry S. Ashmore. *Civil Rights and Wrongs: A Memoir of Race and Politics 1944–1994*. New York: Pantheon Books, 1994, 96–97.
4. Ibid., 97.
5. Virginia Commonwealth University Libraries, *Separate But Not Equal: Race, Education, and Prince Edward County, Virginia*.
6. Jack Bass. *Unlikely Heroes: The Dramatic Story of the Southern Judges of the Fifth Circuit Who Translated the Supreme Court's Brown Decision into a Revolution for Equality*. New York: Simon and Schuster, 1981, 16.
7. Ibid.
8. Ibid.
9. Georgia Archives; Georgia State Constitution of 1945, Article VIII.
10. Ibid., Amendment to Article VIII of State of Georgia Constitution, 1954.
11. *Good Housekeeping*, May 19, 1962, 194.
12. Numan V. Bartley. *The New South 1945–1980*. Baton Rouge: Louisiana State University Press, 1995, 227.
13. Roche, *The Sibley Commission*, 38.
14. Ashmore, *Civil Rights and Wrongs*, 129.
15. Robert Somerlott. *The Little Rock Desegregation Crisis in American History*. Berkeley, NJ: Enslow Publishers, Inc., 2001, 37.
16. Ashmore, *Civil Rights and Wrongs*, 131.
17. Somerlott, *The Little Rock Desegregation Crisis*, 73.
18. Ibid., 78, "Daisy Bates Memoir."
19. Numan V. Bartley. *The New South*, 241.
20. Ibid., 188.
21. Ibid., 189.
22. Roche, *The Sibley Commission*, 39.
23. David R. Goldfield. *Black, White, and Southern: Race Relations and Southern Culture, 1940 to the Present*. Baton Rouge: Louisiana State University Press, 1990, 113.
24. Roche, *The Sibley Commission*, 52.
25. Ronald H. Bayor. *Race and the Shaping of Twentieth-Century Atlanta*. Chapel Hill: The University of North Carolina Press, 1996, 30.
26. Ibid., 30.
27. *Atlanta Constitution*, December 12, 1959.

Chapter 2

1. Gary M. Pomerantz. *Where Peachtree Meets Sweet Auburn: A Saga of Race and Family*. New York: Penguin Books, 1997, 67.
2. Edward Ayers. *The Promise of the New South: Life after Reconstruction*. New York: Oxford University Press, 1992, 21.
3. Numan V. Bartley. *The Creation of Modern Georgia*, 2nd ed. Athens: University of Georgia Press, 1990, 85.
4. Ibid.
5. Writers' Program of the WPA, Georgia. Sponsored by the Atlanta Board of Education. *Atlanta, A City of the Modern South*. New York: Smith & Durrell, 1942, 9.
6. Ibid.
7. Pomerantz, *Where Peachtree Meets Sweet Auburn*, 35–36.
8. Ibid., 40.
9. Ibid., 40–41.
10. Ibid., 49.
11. Writers' Program. *Atlanta, A City of the Modern South*, 23.
12. Pomerantz, *Where Peachtree Meets Sweet Auburn*, 49.
13. Bartley, *The Creation of Modern Georgia*, 54.
14. Pomerantz, *Where Peachtree Meets Sweet Auburn*, 53.
15. Ibid., 53.
16. Ibid., 54.
17. Atlanta Promotional Brochure, 1900, Atlanta History Center Archives.
18. Taylor Branch. *Parting the Waters: America in the King Years, 1954–63*. New York: Simon and Schuster, Inc., 1988, 31.
19. Pomerantz, *Where Peachtree Meets Sweet Auburn*, 73.
20. Ibid.
21. Branch, *Parting the Waters*, 32.

Chapter 3

1. *Atlanta Constitution*, June 3, 1959.
2. Muggsy Smith. "For Sale — Spring Street School" speech, November 18, 1958, HOPE/Lokey papers, Atlanta History Center Archives.

3. Ibid.
4. Ibid.
5. Ibid.
6. Ibid.
7. Ibid.
8. Maxine Friedman. Interview by Rebecca H. Dartt, May 5, 1999.
9. *Atlanta Constitution*, December 3, 1958.
10. Ralph McGill. *The South and the Southerner*. Boston: Little, Brown and Company, 1959, 256.
11. Numan V. Bartley. *The Creation of Modern Georgia*, 2nd ed. Athens: University of Georgia Press, 1990, 28.
12. Kathryn L. Nasstrom. *Everybody's Grandmother & Nobody's Fool: Frances Freeborn Pauley and the Struggle for Social Justice*. Ithaca, NY: Cornell University Press, 2000, 43–44.
13. Calvin Kytle and James A. Mackay. *Who Runs Georgia?* Athens: University of Georgia Press, 1998, 10.
14. William Anderson. *The Wild Man from Sugar Creek: The Political Career of Eugene Talmadge*. Baton Rouge: Louisiana State University Press, 1975, 226.
15. Bartley, *The Creation of Modern Georgia*, 175.
16. Ibid., 194.
17. Ibid., 201.
18. Ibid., 202.
19. Anderson, *The Wild Man*, 205.
20. Bartley, *The Creation of Modern Georgia*, 208.
21. *Saturday Evening Post*, "The Deep South Says Never," June, 1957.

Chapter 4

1. *Atlanta-Journal Constitution*, January 11, 1959.
2. Gary M. Pomerantz. *Where Peachtree Meets Sweet Auburn: A Saga of Race and Family*. New York: Penguin Books, 1997, 273.
3. *Atlanta Constitution*, December 15, 1958.
4. Ibid., "Ministers Manifesto," December 14, 1958.

5. Ibid., December 22, 1958.
6. Ibid.
7. Ibid., November 20, 1958.
8. Ibid.
9. Ibid., January 18, 1959.
10. Ibid., January 10, 1959.
11. Ibid.
12. Ibid.
13. Kathryn L. Nasstrom. *Everybody's Grandmother & Nobody's Fool: Frances Freeborn Pauley and the Struggle for Social Justice.* Ithaca, NY: Cornell University Press, 2000, 38.
14. *Atlanta Constitution,* January 16, 1959.
15. Ibid.
16. Ibid., Celestine Sibley column, January, 1959.
17. Jeff Roche. *Restructured Resistance: The Sibley Commission and the Politics of Desegregation in Georgia.* Athens: The University of Georgia Press, 1998, 49.
18. Ibid.
19. *Atlanta Constitution,* February 10, 1959.

Chapter 5

1. *Atlanta Constitution,* March 29, 1959.
2. Betty Harris. Interview Transcript by Paul T. Mertz, August 20, 1988.
3. Kathryn L. Nasstrom. Speech at Symposium of "The HOPE Story," March 11, 2000, Emory University.
4. Nan Pendergrast. Interview by Rebecca H. Dartt, May 7, 1999.
5. Frances Pauley Papers, "HOPE Organized for Action." Manuscript, Archives and Rare Book Library, Emory University.
6. Fran Breeden. Interview by Rebecca H. Dartt, February 18, 1999.
7. Ibid.
8. Ibid.
9. Ibid.
10. Kathryn L. Nasstrom. *Everybody's Grandmother & Nobody's Fool: Frances Freeborn Pauley and the Struggle for Social Justice.* Ithaca, NY: Cornell University Press, 2000, 59.

11. *Atlanta Constitution,* March 5, 1959.
12. Ibid.
13. Ibid.
14. Ibid.
15. *Atlanta Metropolitan Herald,* March 11, 1959.
16. Ibid.
17. Ibid.
18. *Atlanta Constitution,* March 5, 1959.
19. Ibid.
20. Harry Boyte. Speech at Tower Rally, HOPE/Lokey Papers, Atlanta History Center Archives.
21. Ibid.
22. Ibid.
23. Ibid.
24. Hope/Lokey Papers, Atlanta History Center Archives.

Chapter 6

1. *Atlanta Constitution,* March 29, 1959.
2. Beverly Long (Downing). Interview by Rebecca H. Dartt, May 8, 1999.
3. *Atlanta Journal,* April 2, 1959.
4. Ralph McGill. "The Crisis of the City," *Saturday Review of Literature,* May 23, 1959.
5. Jeff Roche. *Restructured Resistance: The Sibley Commission and the Politics of Desegregation in Georgia.* Athens: The University of Georgia Press, 1998, 60.
6. *Atlanta Journal,* March 9, 1959.
7. Muriel Lokey. Interview by Rebecca H. Dartt, May 7, 1999.
8. HOPE/Lokey papers, Box 1, Atlanta History Center Archives.
9. Roche, *The Sibley Commission,* 61.
10. *Atlanta Constitution,* March 21, 1959.
11. *Augusta Courier,* editorial by Roy Harris, November 9, 1959.
12. Ibid.
13. Nan Pendergrast. Interview by Rebecca H. Dartt, May 7, 1999.
14. *Atlanta Constitution,* June 10, 1959.
15. Ibid.
16. *Atlanta Constitution,* June 8, 1959.
17. Betty Harris. Interview Transcript by Paul T. Mertz, August 20, 1988.

18. Betty Harris. Personal Conversation witnessed by Rebecca H. Dartt.
19. Fran Breeden. Interview by Rebecca H. Dartt, February 18, 1999.
20. Ibid.
21. *Atlanta Journal,* February 8, 1960.
22. Kathryn L. Nasstrom. *Everybody's Grandmother & Nobody's Fool: Frances Freeborn Pauley and the Struggle for Social Justice.* Ithaca, NY: Cornell University Press, 2000, 59.
23. Maxine Friedman. Interview by Rebecca H. Dartt, May 5, 1999.
24. Ibid.

Chapter 7

1. HOPE/Lokey papers, Atlanta History Center Archives.
2. Jeff Roche. *Restructured Resistance: The Sibley Commission and the Politics of Desegregation in Georgia.* Athens: The University of Georgia Press, 1998, 47.
3. A. T. Walden. Papers, Atlanta History Center Archives.
4. Jack Bass. *Unlikely Heroes: The Dramatic Story of the Southern Judges of the Fifth Circuit Who Translated the Supreme Court's Brown Decision into a Revolution for Equality.* New York: Simon and Schuster, 1981, 13–14.
5. Roche, *The Sibley Commission,* 47.
6. *Atlanta Journal,* June 7, 1959.
7. Ibid.
8. Numan V. Bartley. *The Creation of Modern Georgia,* 2nd ed. Athens: University of Georgia Press, 1990, 80.
9. Ibid., 156.
10. Ibid., 155.
11. Ibid., 157.
12. Ibid..
13. Jerry John Thornberry. *The Development of Black Atlanta: History of Atlanta Public Schools,* 1885–1885 [Dissertation], Graduate School of University of Maryland, 1977.
14. Ibid.
15. Ibid.
16. Ibid.
17. Ibid.

18. Ibid.
19. Ibid.
20. Ibid.
21. Ibid.
22. Roche, *The Sibley Commission,* 47.
23. Southern Regional Council, *Will the Circle Be Unbroken,* audio history, *1998.*
24. Roche, *The Sibley Commission,* 47.
25. Roche, *The Sibley Commission,* 47–48.
26. *Atlanta Constitution,* July 18, 1959.
27. David R. Goldfield. *Black, White, and Southern: Race Relations and Southern Culture, 1940 to the Present.* Baton Rouge: Louisiana State University Press, 1990, 113.
28. Eliza Paschall. Papers, "Reprint of Atlanta Board of Education Desegregation Plan," Manuscript, Archives and Rare Book Library, Emory University.

Chapter 8

1. Jeff Roche. *Restructured Resistance: The Sibley Commission and the Politics of Desegregation in Georgia.* Athens: The University of Georgia Press, 1998, 85.
2. Ibid., 81–82.
3. Beverly Long (Downing). Interview by Rebecca H. Dartt, May 8, 1999.
4. Ibid.
5. Fran Breeden. Interview by Rebecca H. Dartt, February 18, 1999.
6. Roche, *The Sibley Commission,* 83–84.
7. Ibid., 83.
8. Ibid., 83–84.
9. Fran Breeden. Interview by Rebecca H. Dartt, February 18, 1999.
10. Betty Harris. Interview Transcript by Paul T. Mertz, August 20, 1988.
11. HOPE/Lokey Papers, Atlanta History Center Archives.
12. Ibid.
13. Kathryn L. Nasstrom. *Everybody's Grandmother & Nobody's Fool: Frances Freeborn Pauley and the Struggle for Social Justice.* Ithaca, NY: Cornell University Press, 2000, 57–58.
14. *Atlanta Constitution,* January 10, 1960.

15. Roche, *The Sibley Commission,* 83–84.
16. Ibid.
17. Ibid., 85.
18. Ibid., 89.
19. Ibid., 86.
20. Ibid., 89.
21. Ibid.
22. Ibid., 90–91.
23. HOPE/Lokey Papers, Atlanta History Center Archives.

Chapter 9

1. Paul T. Mertz. *Georgia Historical Quarterly,* Spring 1993, 57.
2. Jeff Roche. *Restructured Resistance: The Sibley Commission and the Politics of Desegregation in Georgia.* Athens: The University of Georgia Press, 1998, 94.
3. Ibid., 100.
4. Ibid., 101.
5. Ibid., 103.
6. Ibid.
7. Ibid., 104–105.
8. Betty Harris. Interview Transcript by Paul T. Mertz, August 20, 1988.
9. Roche, *The Sibley Commission,* 105.
10. Kathryn L. Nasstrom. *Everybody's Grandmother & Nobody's Fool: Frances Freeborn Pauley and the Struggle for Social Justice.* Ithaca, NY: Cornell University Press, 2000, 60.
11. Roche, *The Sibley Commission,* 105.
12. Ibid.
13. Betty Harris. Interview Transcript by Paul T. Mertz, August 20, 1988.
14. Roche, *The Sibley Commission,* 106.
15. Nasstrom, *Everybody's Grandmother,* 60–61.
16. Roche, *The Sibley Commission,* 107.
17. Ibid., 122.
18. Ibid., 124.
19. Ibid., 107.
20. Ibid., 115.
21. Ibid.

Chapter 10

1. Betty Harris. Interview Transcript by Paul T. Mertz, August 10, 1988.

2. Jeff Roche. *Restructured Resistance: The Sibley Commission and the Politics of Desegregation in Georgia.* Athens: The University of Georgia Press, 1998, 124–125.
3. Ibid., 126.
4. Ibid., 130.
5. Ibid., 132.
6. Ibid.
7. Ibid., 134.
8. Ibid., 140.
9. Ibid., 141.
10. Ibid., 142.
11. Ibid., 144.
12. *Atlanta Constitution,* March 22, 1960.
13. Roche, *The Sibley Commission,* 145.
14. Ibid., 146.
15. Ibid., 147.
16. Fran Breeden. Interview by Rebecca H. Dartt, February 18, 1999.
17. Nan Pendergrast. Interview by Rebecca H. Dartt, May, 7, 1999.
18. Roche, *The Sibley Commission,* 150.
19. Ibid., 151
20. Ibid., 151–152.
21. Ibid., 155.
22. Ibid., 162.

Chapter 11

1. *Atlanta Constitution,* May 10, 1960.
2. Lucy Huie. Symposium on "Story of HOPE," March 11, 2000, Emory University.
3. Ibid.
4. Jeff Roche. *Restructured Resistance: The Sibley Commission and the Politics of Desegregation in Georgia.* Athens: The University of Georgia Press, 1998, 163.
5. Ibid., Sibley's majority report, 163–166.
6. Ibid., 166–167.
7. *Atlanta Constitution,* May 10, 1960.
8. Ibid.
9. Ibid.
10. Numan V. Bartley. *The New South 1945–1980.* Baton Rouge: Louisiana State University Press, 1995, 250.
11. Ibid., 251–252.

12. *Atlanta Constitution*, May 10, 1960.
13. Ibid.
14. Roche, *The Sibley Commission*, 170.
15. Ibid.
16. HOPE/Lokey Papers, "HOPE 1960 Yearly Report," Atlanta History Center Archives.
17. HOPE/Lokey Papers, Atlanta History Center Archives.
18. Roche, *The Sibley Commission*, 172–173.
19. Beverly Long (Downing). Interview by Rebecca H. Dartt, May 8, 1999.
20. Roche, *The Sibley Commission*, 173.
21. Ibid., 174–175.
22. *Macon Telegraph,* November 12, 1960.
23. Numan V. Bartley. *The New South*, 252.
24. HOPE/Lokey Papers, Atlanta History Center Archives.
25. Ibid.
26. Roche, *The Sibley Commission*, 178.
27. Ibid., 173.
28. Ibid., 173–174.

Chapter 12

1. *Atlanta Constitution,* January 12, 1961.
2. James Welden Jr. Symposium, "Story of HOPE," March 11, 2000, Emory University.
3. *The Red and Black* (University of Georgia Newspaper), January 9, 1961.
4. Calvin Trillin. *An Education in Georgia: The Integration of Charlayne Hunter and Hamilton Holmes*. New York: The Viking Press, 1964, 51.
5. Jeff Roche. *Restructured Resistance: The Sibley Commission and the Politics of Desegregation in Georgia*. Athens: The University of Georgia Press, 1998, 179.
6. Jack Bass. *Unlikely Heroes: The Dramatic Story of the Southern Judges of the Fifth Circuit Who Translated the Supreme Court's Brown Decision into a Revolution for Equality*. New York: Simon and Schuster, 1981, 31, 53.
7. Judge James Barrow and Phyllis

Barrow. Interview by Rebecca H. Dartt, May 10, 1999.
8. Ibid.
9. Roche, *The Sibley Commission*, 179–80.
10. Ibid., 180.
11. Ibid.
12. Betty Harris. Interview Transcript by Paul T. Mertz, August 20, 1988.
13. *Good Housekeeping*, May, 1962.
14. Roche, *The Sibley Commission*, 180.
15. Ibid., 181.
16. Ibid.
17. Ibid.
18. Ibid., 182.
19. Ibid.
20. Ibid.
21. *Atlanta Constitution,* January 19, 1961.
22. Kathryn L. Nasstrom. *Everybody's Grandmother & Nobody's Fool: Frances Freeborn Pauley and the Struggle for Social Justice*. Ithaca, NY: Cornell University Press, 2000, 61.
23. *Atlanta Constitution,* January 19, 1961.
24. Judge James Barrow and Phyllis Barrow, Interview by Rebecca H. Dartt, May 10, 1999.

Chapter 13

1. Madelyn Nix. Symposium on "Story of HOPE," March 11, 2000, Emory University.
2. *Look,* May 25, 1961.
3. HOPE/Lokey Papers, Atlanta History Center Archives.
4. Ruby Bridges. *Through My Eyes,* New York: Scholastic Press, 1999, 12.
5. Madelyn Nix, Symposium on "Story of HOPE."
6. Tom Welch. Interview by Virginie Thiriot, 1991.
7. Tom Welch. Interview by Rebecca H. Dartt, April 20, 2002.
8. Janet Ferguson. Interview Rebecca H. Dartt, May 7, 1999.
9. Betty Harris. Interview Transcript by Paul T. Mertz, August 20, 1988.

Chapter 14

1. Radio communication in Atlanta City Hall, August 30, 1961. HOPE/Lokey Papers, Atlanta History Center Archives.

2. *Atlanta Constitution,* August 31, 1961.

3. *Atlanta Daily World,* August 31, 1961.

4. Madelyn Nix. Symposium on "Story of HOPE," Emory University, March 11, 2000.

5. *Atlanta Constitution,* August 31, 1961.

6. Ibid.

7. Betty Vinson. "Report from City Hall," August 30, 1961. HOPE/Lokey Papers, Atlanta History Center Archives.

8. *Atlanta Daily World,* August 31, 1961.

9. Vinson, "Report from City Hall," August 30, 1961.

10. *Atlanta Constitution,* August 31, 1961.

11. Ibid.

12. Ibid.

13. HOPE/Lokey papers, Atlanta History Center Archives.

Epilogue

1. Maxine Friedman. Interview by Rebecca H. Dartt, May 5, 1999.

2. Fran Breeden. Interview by Rebecca H. Dartt, February 18, 1999.

3. Nan Pendergrast. Interview by Rebecca H. Dartt, May 7, 1999.

4. *The New Georgia Encyclopedia, Government and Politics,* www.georgiaencyclopedia.org.

5. *Our Georgia History.com;* Biography of Judge Frank A. Hooper.

6. Biography of Donald Hollowell, Auburn Avenue Research Library on African-American Culture and History, Atlanta, Georgia.

7. Tom Welch. Interview by Rebecca H. Dartt, April 20, 2002.

8. *Atlanta Journal-Constitution,* August 30, 1991.

9. Ibid.

10. Michael Janofsky. "A New Hope for Dreams Suspended," *New York Times,* July 31, 2005.

11. *Sarasota Herald-Tribune,* February 24, 2007.

Bibliography

Books

Anderson, William. *The Wild Man from Sugar Creek: The Political Career of Eugene Talmadge*. Baton Rouge: Louisiana State University Press, 1975.

Ashmore, Harry S. *An Epitaph for Dixie*, New York: W.W. Norton and Company Inc., 1958.

Ashmore, Harry S. *Civil Rights and Wrongs: A Memoir of Race and Politics 1944–1994*. New York: Pantheon Books, 1994.

Ayers, Edward L. *The Promise of the New South: Life after Reconstruction*. New York: Oxford University Press, 1992.

Bartley, Numan V. *The Creation of Modern Georgia*, 2nd ed. Athens: University of Georgia Press, 1990.

Bartley, Numan V. *The New South 1945–1980*. Baton Rouge: Louisiana State University Press, 1995.

Bartley, Numan V. and Graham, Hugh D. *Southern Politics and the Second Reconstruction*. Baltimore: The John Hopkins University Press, 1975.

Bass, Jack. *Unlikely Heroes: The Dramatic Story of the Southern Judges of the Fifth Circuit Who Translated the Supreme Court's Brown Decision into a Revolution for Equality*. New York: Simon and Schuster, 1981.

Bayor, Ronald H. *Race and the Shaping of Twentieth-Century Atlanta*. Chapel Hill: The University of North Carolina Press, 1996.

Belknap, Michal R. *Federal Law and Southern Order: Racial Violence and Constitutional Conflict in the Post-Brown South*. Athens, GA: The University of Georgia Press, 1987.

Black, Earl. *Southern Governors and Civil Rights*. Cambridge: Harvard University Press, 1976.

Branch, Taylor. *Parting the Waters: America in the King Years, 1954–63*. New York: Simon and Schuster, Inc., 1988.

Bridges, Ruby. *Through My Eyes*. New York: Scholastic Press, 1999.

Cash, W. J. *The Mind of the South*. New York: Alfred K. Knopf, 1941.

Clotfelter, Charles T. *The Rise and Retreat of School Desegregation*. Princeton, NJ: Princeton University Press, 2004.

Egerton, John. *Speak Now against the Day: The Generation before the Civil Rights Movement in the South*. Chapel Hill: University of North Carolina Press, 1995.

Fite, Gilbert C. *Richard B. Russell, Jr., Senator from Georgia*. Chapel Hill: University of North Carolina Press, 1991.

Goldfield, David R. *Black, White, and Southern: Race Relations and Southern Culture, 1940 to the Present*. Baton Rouge: Louisiana State University Press, 1990.

Grant, Donald L. *The Way It Was in the South: The Black Experience in Georgia*. Secausus, NJ: Carol Pub. Group, 1993.

Henderson, Harold Paulk. *Ernest Vandiver: Governor of Georgia*. Athens: University of Georgia Press, 2000.

Hunter-Gault, Charlayne, *In My Place*. New York: Farrar Straus Giroux, 1992.

Kytle, Calvin and Mackay, James A. *Who Runs Georgia?* Athens: University of Georgia Press, 1998.

McGill, Ralph. *The South and the Southerner*. Boston: Little, Brown and Company, 1959.

Nasstrom, Kathryn L. *Everybody's Grandmother & Nobody's Fool: Frances Freeborn Pauley and the Struggle for Social Justice*. Ithaca, NY: Cornell University Press, 2000.

Pomerantz, Gary M. *Where Peachtree Meets Sweet Auburn: A Saga of Race and Family*. New York: Penguin Books, 1997.

Roche, Jeff. *Restructured Resistance: The Sibley Commission and the Politics of Desegregation in Georgia*. Athens: The University of Georgia Press, 1998.

Somerlott, Robert. *The Little Rock Desegregation Crisis in American History*. Berkeley, NJ: Enslow Publishers, Inc., 2001.

Thornberry, Jerry John. *The Development of Black Atlanta: History of Atlanta Public Schools, 1865–1885* [Dissertation], Graduate School of University of Maryland, 1977.

Trillin, Calvin. *An Education in Georgia: The Integration of Charlayne Hunter and Hamilton Holmes*. New York: The Viking Press, 1964.

Writers' Program of the WPA, Georgia. Sponsored by the Atlanta Board of Education. *Atlanta, A City of the Modern South*. New York: Smith & Durrell, 1942.

Newspapers

Atlanta Constitution
Atlanta Journal
Augusta Courier

Bainbridge Post-Searchlight
Calhoun Times
Macon Telegraph
New York Times
The Red and Black (University of Georgia)
Sarasota Herald-Tribune

Periodicals

Georgia Historical Quarterly
Good Housekeeping
Life
Look
Saturday Review
Time

Interviews

Barrow, Judge James and Phyllis Barrow. Interview by Rebecca H. Dartt, May 10, 1999.
Breeden, Fran. Interview by Rebecca H. Dartt, February 18, 1999.
Ferguson, Janet. Interview by Rebecca H. Dartt, May 7, 1999.
Friedman, Maxine. Interview by Rebecca H. Dartt, May 5, 1999.
Harris, Betty. Interview by Paul T. Mertz, August 20, 1988.
Lokey, Muriel. Interview by Rebecca H. Dartt, May 6, 1999.
Long, Beverly. Interview by Rebecca H. Dartt, May 8, 1999.
Nix-Beamen, Madelyn. Interview by Rebecca H. Dartt, April 17, 2002.
Pauley, Frances. Interview by Rebecca H. Dartt, May 6, 1999.
Pendergrast, Nan. Interview by Rebecca H. Dartt, May 7, 1999.
Welch, Tom. Interview by Rebecca H. Dartt, April 19, 2002.
Welch, Tom. Interview by Virginie Thiriot, 1991.

Special Collections

Hollowell, Donald, Papers. Auburn Avenue Research Library on African-American Culture and History, Atlanta, Georgia.
HOPE/Lokey, Muriel, Papers. Atlanta History Center Archives, Atlanta, Georgia.
Pauley, Frances, Papers. Emory University Robert W. Woodruff Library, Atlanta, Georgia.
Pascal, Eliza, Papers. Emory University Robert W. Woodruff Library, Atlanta, Georgia.
Walden, A. T., Papers. Atlanta History Center Archives, Atlanta, Georgia.

Other Sources

Emory University Symposium and Panel Discussion, "Desegregating Schools in Atlanta, 1954–1964: The Story of HOPE," March 11, 2000 [taped transcript].
Georgia Archives, Atlanta, Georgia.
New Georgia Encyclopedia, Government and Politics. www.georgiaencyclope dia.org
Our Georgia History (website). www.ourgeorgiahistory.com.
Peeples, Edward H., *Separate but Not Equal: Race, Education, and Prince Edward County, Virginia*, online exhibit. Virginia Commonwealth University Libraries, www.library.vcu.edu/jbc/speccoll/pec.html
Southern Regional Council, *Will the Circle be Unbroken*, An audio history of the Civil Rights Movement in five Southern communities and the music of those times, 1998.

Index